THE U.S. GOVERNMENT WASTES AT LEAST $375 BILLION

W9-BNV-035

Eliminating that could mean a 40 percent cut in your personal income tax!

Our nation's politicians are not only spending a "surplus" that mainly does not exist, but they treat our taxes in a cavalier, non-sensical fashion.

- Earned Income Tax Credits—including checks—go to people who make over $30,000 a year, which is more than the average wage earner.

- PORK eats up $15 billion a year, including $104,000 to study how people communicate through facial expressions.

- Despite supposed welfare reform, welfare is our largest national expenditure. At last count, it costs $400 billion a year through 81 different programs, with no central computer.

- We pay $600 million a year to subsidize peanut farmers who have an exclusive federal "quota" license going back to the 1930s.

- One in eight Small Business Administration defaulted loans were made to convicted criminals.

- HUD overpaid landlords $900 million in rental subsidies in one year.

- The General Services Administration spent $121 million on a computer system that didn't work.

- Taxpayers paid $26 million for the 2000 presidential conventions—including liquor and entertainment. And we weren't even invited.

PLUS MORE WASTE THAN YOU CAN IMAGINE AND A
PLAN TO REMAKE A DYSFUNCTIONAL WASHINGTON

Also by Martin L. Gross

Nonfiction

The Conspiracy of Ignorance:
The Failure of American Public Schools

The Medical Racket:
How Doctors, HMOs, and Hospitals Are Failing
the American Patient

The End of Sanity:
Social and Cultural Madness in America

The Government Racket:
Washington Waste from A to Z

A Call for Revolution:
How Washington Is Strangling America

The Political Racket:
Deceit, Self-Interest and Corruption in American Politics

The Tax Racket

The Psychological Society

The Brain Watchers

The Doctors

Fiction

Man of Destiny

THE
GOVERNMENT
RACKET

2000 AND BEYOND

MARTIN L. GROSS

Quill

An Imprint of HarperCollinsPublishers

THE GOVERNMENT RACKET 2000 AND BEYOND. Copyright © 2000, 2001 by Martin L. Gross. All rights reserved. Printed in the United States of America. No part of this book may be used or reproduced in any manner whatsoever without written permission except in the case of brief quotations embodied in critical articles and reviews. For information address Harper-Collins Publishers Inc., 10 East 53rd Street, New York, NY 10022.

HarperCollins books may be purchased for educational, business, or sales promotional use. For information please write: Special Markets Department, HarperCollins Publishers Inc., 10 East 53rd Street, New York, NY 10022.

First Quill edition published 2001.

Library of Congress Cataloging-in-Publication Data is available.
ISBN 0-06-093394-1

01 02 03 04 05 ❖/RRD 10 9 8 7 6 5 4 3 2 1

To my wife, Anita

and
To Thomas Jefferson
from whom all liberty springs

Contents

INTRODUCTION   1

Part One
NEW WASHINGTON WASTE

1   ACCOUNTING   9
    Is There a Bookkeeper in the House?

2   BABY-SITTERS, WASHINGTON STYLE   16
    "But I Don't Need Welfare!"

3   BUDGET   19
    *How to Steal $6 Trillion from Social Security
    and Call It a "Surplus"*

4   COMPUTERS   31
    WANTED: Teenage Hackers

5   CONVENTIONS, PRESIDENTIAL   38
    They're Partying on Our Nickel

6   CORPORATE WELFARE   41
     You Mean I'm Subsidizing Intel?

7   DEMONSTRATION PROJECTS   49
     Highways to Pork Heaven

8   EARNED INCOME TAX CREDIT (EITC)   57
     *Are You Getting Your Free Money from
     Uncle Sam?*

9   FEDERAL FOLLIES   65
     More Aggravating Than Entertaining

10   FEDERAL PALACES   72
     $13 Million Just for the Architect?

11   GOLF   78
     Putts Instead of Planes

12   HORSES   81
     Millions for Belgian Steaks

13   INTERNATIONAL ENTERPRISE FUNDS   84
     Want to Buy a Mutual Fund—in Bulgaria?

14   JUNKETS, MILITARY STYLE   89
     Fly Me to the Moon

15   KICKBACKS, BRIBES, CON JOBS, AND SIMPLE
     FRAUD   93
     Uncle Sucker Gets Ripped Off, Inside and Out

16   LOANS   106
     The Government Bank: Everyone's Welcome

17   MASS TRANSIT   110
     Brother, Can You Spare Train Fare?

18   MERCHANT MARINE   115
     What Happened to Old Glory at Sea?

19 METRIC SYSTEM   121
    How Many Millimeters Long Is Your Foot?

20 NATIONAL PARKS   125
    Purple Mountain Majesty and Red Ink

21 NATIVE AMERICANS   129
    Gambling Casinos: Revenge on the Palefaces

22 OUTHOUSES   135
    Relief Is Just a Fortune Away

23 PEANUTS   137
    Want to Buy Some Bootleg Nuts?

24 PORK   141
    *$15 Billion a Year to Study Why Politicians Are
    Compulsive Spenders*

25 QUAKES, HURRICANES, FEMA, AND OTHER
    DISASTERS   155
    We Insure Everything

26 RADIO ADS   160
    Are We Paying to Pollute the Airwaves?

27 RECORDING STUDIOS   163
    High Tech—in Your Face

28 SMALL-BUSINESS CRIMINALS   167
    Holding Up Uncle Sam

29 SSI—SUPPLEMENTAL SECURITY INCOME   171
    A Good Idea Too Often Gone Bad

30 STATISTICAL SERVICES   181
    They've Got Our Number—Seventy-three Times

31 TELEPHONES   185
    Just Charge It to Uncle Sam

32 UNIVERSAL SERVICE FUND   190
    Reach Out and Touch Someone—Like Harrison Ford

33 VOLUNTEERS (AMERICORPS)   193
    In Washington They Get Paid

34 WELFARE   197
    It's Bigger Than You Think

35 YOUTH AT RISK   204
    Have I Got a Teen Program for You!

36 ZOOMING NATIONAL DEBT   208
    It Still Goes Only One Way—Up

Part Two
REVIEW AND DÉJÀ VU
Defeats and Victories in the Fight Against Waste

Office of Former Speakers   216
Government Airplanes, Nonmilitary   217
Decorating for the Bureaucracy   219
Helium   221
Congressional LSOs   222
Mining Law of 1872   223
Wool and Mohair   226
Rural Utilities Services   227
Essential Air   229
Federal Employees   231
Congressional Retirement   235
Auctioning Off the Airwaves   237
Newsletters   238
Forest Service—More Corporate Welfare   240
Congressional Perks   242

PART THREE
BLUEPRINT FOR THE TWENTY-FIRST CENTURY
*How to Redesign the Government and
Save a Fortune in the Process*

The Cabinet	254
The Oversized Little Cabinet	260
Programs That Should Be Eliminated	261
Antisubsidy Act	262
Duplication and Overlap	262
Congress	264
Presidential Primaries	268
Taxes: Eliminate the Internal Revenue Service	272
Initiative and Referendum	274
Establish an Independent Inspector General of the United States	277
APPENDIX	281
An Inventory of Waste: What's the Total?	
INDEX	285

Introduction

My book *The Government Racket: Washington Waste from A to Z* accomplished much of what I had hoped for.

Published in the summer of 1992, it reached near the top of the *New York Times* bestseller list and helped alert the nation to the fact that the federal government is too often dysfunctional when it comes to waste and efficiency. Regularly, it appears, they spend our tax money with wild abandon.

Five times I have testified before Senate and House committees about serious flaws in the Washington operation—from excess staffing to overhead, failed programs from job training to ludicrous corporate subsidies, and even the overgenerous giving away of the nation's mineral treasures.

In 1994 the nation was so annoyed at the condition of the federal government that they changed their traditional politics, electing a Republican majority in both houses of Congress for the first time in forty-two years.

That new Congress initially marched to the step of the people's drum, promising radical change. They would reduce taxes substantially, balance the budget, close unwanted cabinet and other agencies, cut out flagrant waste. And they wouldn't use a fine scalpel but a forester's broad ax.

Smaller government and the elimination of waste soon became the war chant of what was billed as a "revolution" in Washington. The challenge was first met by Democrats with antagonism, but they quickly decided that it was wise to join, not fight, the revolution. The President took up the call and in his State of the Union address trumpeted that "THE ERA OF BIG GOVERNMENT IS OVER"—a happy theme greeted with a cheer reminiscent of a winning home run in the ninth inning of a Yankees game.

Unfortunately, the reality is quite different. That statement, whether chanted by followers of the Donkey or the Elephant, has turned out to be one of the great bipartisan lies of all times. Big government is not only intact and healthy, but is bigger and more robust than ever before.

The cost of the federal government will pass $2 trillion in 2001 and an enormous expansion of spending is already in effect. Congressional Budget Office projections show that the government grew 7 percent between 1999 and 2000 and will grow 4 percent per year for the next decade, double the rate of inflation. That is, *if* spending caps are held in place—and *if* that has already been eliminated by the 2000 and 2001 budgets.

Washington's tax bite now takes a larger percentage of the gross domestic product than at any time in the history of the nation.

American politicians regularly demonstrate their indifference to the financial health of citizens while they zealously guard their own pocketbooks with extravagant pay raises and fattened retirement checks.

Overall, according to the Tax Foundation, the tax burden on the typical citizen has reached over $10,000 for every man, woman, and child. The average family now pays more in taxes than they spend for food, housing, and medical care combined.

The local and state burden is almost as oppressive as Washington's. That tariff is now up to $3,129 per person, three times in real dollars what it was in 1960. "Tax Freedom Day," which is when we stop working for *all* governments and start working for ourselves keeps rising rapidly. It is now in May nationally and into the latter part of the month in Connecticut and New York.

Despite all the talk about federal tax cuts, millions of Americans get an automatic *increase* each year as the income "limit" on which we pay FICA taxes rises. That figure has skyrocketed from $57,600 in 1993 to $76,200 in 2000, an increase of some 6 *percent per year*, adding some $1,000 to the current annual tax bill of salaried employees in that bracket, and almost $2,000 for the self-employed, a hidden tax increase no politician talks about.

Has it always been this way? Hardly.

The total cost of government (federal, state, and local) under FDR, who was supposedly a big spender, was 17 percent of the gross domestic product. Under Harry Truman it was only 22 percent, and it didn't reach 30 percent until the days of Lyndon Johnson. Today, taxes take almost 38 percent of the GDP, and rises each year.

It might interest boomers to know that a typical single-earner family today is paying almost *three times* as much of their income (in real dollars) to Washington as their parents did in 1950. No wonder it seemed like, and was, the good old days.

And waste continues to flow like a swollen river across a floodplain. But, you might ask, how can this be? The budget is balanced and we are ostensibly racking up enormous surpluses—$70 billion in fiscal 1998 alone, $123 billion in 1999, rising to $237 billion in 2000, then to an astronomical $444 billion in 2009, for a total of $3.02 *trillion* by the end of the next decade, according to the Congressional Budget Office.

And aren't the number crunchers in the White House projecting more than a $4 trillion "surplus" over the next fifteen years?

Good question, but I fear that the truthful answer is diametrically opposed to the barrage of propaganda issued daily from the nation's capital.

And why have I put quote marks around the word "surplus"?

Only because, as we shall later see in detail, 100 percent of the supposed "surplus" was money "borrowed" from Social Security in 1998 and 1999, and three-fourths of it in 2000. (See Chapter 3, Budget.)

I propose to expose this unconscionable hoax using the government's own figures and quoting its more honest voices.

Of course, most of this book is devoted to waste and how to clean it up. We will witness the failed halfhearted attempt over the last eight years to cut out crippling, unnecessary spending. Not only has it not been cut, but it has increased and can now be measured at some $375 billion a year—without damaging social welfare programs, including Medicare and Social Security.

If we could put in a true cost-cutting program as the public hoped, and expected, we would save enough money to give more than a 40 percent tax cut to those who file the IRS Form 1040, which brought in $863 billion in fiscal 1999 from salaries, royalties, and capital gains.

The Republican majority trumpeted a similar goal when they took over Congress in 1995, claiming that scores of large inefficient programs would be eliminated, including four major cabinet agencies: Energy, Commerce, Education, and Housing and Urban Development. All four, of course, are still standing and three have received *increases* in their budgets.

In Part One of this volume (New Washington Waste), we will look at a host (36) of newly described areas of waste. And in Part Two (Review and Déjà Vu), we will revisit several of those I first exposed in 1992, showing a handful of taxpayer victories along with a longer list of defeats in the war against waste.

Even the so-called welfare reform (see Chapter 34, Welfare) will be seen as hollow rhetoric, resulting in increased costs to taxpayers as clients ostensibly leave the rolls.

In Part Three of the book (Blueprint for the Twenty-first Century), we will attempt a major reorganization of the entire federal government so that the perpetrators of inefficiency and ignorant administration will find it more difficult to fool the public.

Finally in the Appendix, we will catalog the waste enumerated in this volume, convinced there is still much more hidden in the bowels of Washington.

To the hope that this second look at federal waste will enrage the public sufficiently for politicians to cut the size of the often foolish government and reform it on behalf of the citizenry, this book is lovingly dedicated.

Over two hundred years ago, James Madison warned us about an "oligarchy" in the Federal District (Washington, D.C.) that could result from an overcentralized, oversized government run by politicians. His prophecy was accurate, and we face that threat today, one that cramps both democracy and our pocketbooks.

Please follow me into the miasma of Washington to gain an intimate look at a *new* inventory of Washington waste, from A to Z, the by-product of a cavalier federal government.

PART ONE

NEW WASHINGTON WASTE

A

1

Accounting

Is There a Bookkeeper in the House?

The citizen made an innocent error on his tax returns and was hounded for months by the Internal Revenue Service, whose bureaucrats compulsively try to collect the last dollar, including exorbitant penalties, from harried taxpayers.

But how is the IRS—and for that matter, the rest of the government—doing with its own internal accounting?

Miserably, say audits of the government's books. Take the IRS. Not only are they hopelessly sloppy with their accounting, but there are funds they can't find, payments made by them that were not valid, and giant chasms in the reconciliation of their own budget.

Some of the IRS accounting errors border on the hilarious, or tragic, depending on your view:

- **A video terminal was listed in IRS inventory as worth $5.6 million. Actual cost? Just $750.**

- The IRS paid $36,000 on a maintenance contract for a microcomputer. There was only one problem. The device had been idle for three years.

- A check of 280 IRS payments to vendors found that 32 of them were duplicate payments. In just that small sample of bills IRS bookkeepers had sent out an extra $500,000.

But is government accounting mayhem restricted to the IRS, the violators of their own warning to taxpayers to be accurate? Hardly.

The Grace Commission reported years ago that the federal government was using 322 different incompatible and apparently irreconcilable accounting systems. New proof of that charge marks Washington as not only the biggest business in the world but the financially sloppiest.

A two-year study of the federal books by the General Accounting Office in 1998 discovered that virtually the entire government is awash in bad bookkeeping, even at the most elemental level.

In their survey of twenty-four cabinet-level and independent government agencies, the GAO found that *only eight* passed muster. The rest were plagued with "significant financial systems weaknesses, problems with fundamental record keeping, incomplete documentation, and weak internal controls."

Take the military. They found that billions of dollars worth of property and equipment could not be sustantiated. The Navy underestimated the value of its property by $10.8 billion. The Air Force could not account for fifteen misplaced jet engines. Says the report: "Certain recorded military property had, in fact, been sold or disposed of in prior years—or could not be located—and an estimated $9 billion of known military operating materials and supplies were not reported."

Other fiscal fiascos in the military were turned up by a separate study of the Pentagon's Defense Finance and Accounting Service (DFAS):

- A DFAS Center in Indianapolis, entrusted with handling a $20 million debt relief program for Desert Storm vets, gave away $15 million—but either to the wrong soldiers or for the wrong debts.

- A soldier's separation check for $183.69 suddenly metamorphosed into one for $836,919.19. By the time Army investigators caught up with him, he had spent almost half the money.

- At another military accounting base, a group of finance clerks created six fictitious soldiers and embezzled their salaries. The clerks even promoted them and sent them worldwide to pad the fraudulent checks.

To return to the IRS, a General Accounting Office audit came to a chilling conclusion about that agency's principal financial statements. The IRS, said the GAO, "has not kept its own books and records with the same degree of accuracy it expects of taxpayers." They could not verify $3 billion of the IRS expenses. "Hundreds of millions of difference have been identified" between what the IRS and the Treasury Department records show, lamented the GAO.

Total revenues of $1.4 trillion and refunds of $233 billion "could not be verified or reconciled." Translation? The IRS numbers did not add up.

Worse yet, the amount collected for various kinds of taxes,

such as Social Security, excise, and personal income taxes, "could not be substantiated."

This unprecedented report came as a result of the Chief Financial Officers Act, which, *for the first time in history*, required the Treasury Department to prepare a consolidated financial statement subject to an independent audit. That, of course, is something American business has been doing for a century or more.

To the innocent eye, a recent "Consolidated Financial Statements of the United States Government" looked impressive and solid, with figures that *supposedly* added up—much like the balance sheet of any corporation, albeit one with a budget of $1.8 *trillion*.

Via column after column of numbers, the report laid out the saga of the government's assets, expenditures, and liabilities. The report would prove to be, Secretary of Treasury Robert E. Rubin assured us, "an important management tool for policy-makers and the public."

A bold statement, but it was more myth than reality. In a shorter audit of only sixteen pages, the General Accounting Office unmercifully ripped the report apart.

In a candid statement, the GAO's chief accountant, Philip T. Calder, scolded the government for "having problems with fundamental recordkeeping" that "prevent the government from accurately reporting *a large portion* [emphasis mine] of its assets, liabilities and costs."

The federal government, the GAO lamented, could:

- Not properly account for billions in property, equipment, materials, and supplies.

- Not properly estimate the cost of federal credit programs and loan guarantees.

- Not determine the real cost of retirement health benefits, veterans benefits, accounts payable, and other liabilities.

- Not accurately report the net cost of government operations.

- Not determine improper payments that run into billions annually.

- Not account for billions of dollars in transactions between government agencies.

Indeed, the official U.S. financial statement was so bad that the GAO refused to confirm its accuracy. Instead, the auditors said that since they could not "determine the reliability" of the information, they were offering no opinion.

The IRS and Defense Department are surely out to lunch when it comes to their bookkeeping, but other agencies are equally indifferent to the manner in which they handle your tax money.

- Because of bookkeeping failure, the Department of Housing and Urban Development paid out $900 million more in Section 8 rental subsidies to landlords than it should have.

- The Federal Aviation Administration's records of $5.5 billion in property and equipment included $195 million in supposed assets that no longer existed. Meanwhile $245 million in spare parts were missing from their books.

- The Forest Service couldn't figure out the correct amount or cost of an estimated $7.8 billion in on-hand property.

- The government loan program, both direct loans and bank guarantees from various agencies, was in total disarray. Washington reported $156 billion in loans receivable and $37 billion in losses for expected defaults. But, says the GAO, there was no evidence that these figures were real. They "should be used with caution," said the auditors, implying that the losses were gravely understated.

- The Department of Education lacked "a reasonable methodology and system" that made it impossible to figure the losses incurred on student loans made and guaranteed by the Department—an amount that runs over $3 billion a year.

- Social Security's bookkeeping was so bad that recipients were overpaid more than $3.1 billion. Just in 1998, $1.2 billion in wasted overpayments was discovered. The government is unlikely to collect more than 15 percent of the overpayments.

- When it came to environmental cleanup, Washington reported their liability as $212 billion, a number the GAO found to be "materially understated."

- The same shortfall was true of the $2.2 trillion for federal employee and veterans' benefits.

When it came to running the government on over $2 trillion a year in 2001 ($2.016 trillion), the GAO was also skeptical, pointing out that there is $100 billion in "unreconciled transactions" that the Treasury cannot figure out because of the "government's inability to properly identify and eliminate transactions between federal government entities . . ."

It's a sorry tale that fits better into a Gilbert and Sullivan comic opera than the modern world of finance.

Washington wonders why people have so little faith in their government. One suspects that not only are the figures askew, but there is the real possibility that the books are regularly cooked to please the bureaucrats and politicians who run, and ruin, the show.

Fortunately, within the morass, there is a possible solution:

The community college in my area will soon be graduating a new crop of young twenty-year-olds in business administration, who surely could go to Washington and clear up the mess.

Meanwhile, is there a *bookkeeper* in the House?

B

2

Baby-sitters, Washington Style
"But I Don't Need Welfare!"

In a suburb of Portland, Oregon, the relatively affluent parents of two young boys needed a baby-sitting service to take care of the kids during the day. Rather than have someone untrained come in, they decided to leave the children with a licensed profit-making day-care home where the woman of the house took care of six children for a price.

It wasn't cheap, but they were satisfied with the quality of the care. They were also satisfied with the price. They asked: "How much extra for food for the children—you know, breakfast, lunch, and a snack?"

The child-care provider smiled. "Oh, don't worry about that. The government pays for that."

"The government? Why? We do pretty well," the father told the woman. "Why should the government feed our children?"

She explained that as a licensed day-care provider, she gets money from Washington through the states, for all the children she cares for—poor, middle-class, or rich. It was all part of the

Child and Adult Care Food Program (CACFP) of the Department of Agriculture, which is administered by the states.

Is it all petty cash? Hardly. The program costs $1.5 billion, which includes nonprofit child-care and adult-care centers, and feeds 2.4 million children and a handful of adults.

Some parts of the program are sensible, but the baby-sitting Family Day Care Home program that feeds the two young Oregon boys is a strange twist without logic—as are so many Washington inventions.

Why? *Because it gives money to both profit-making businesses and children not in need—breaking two rules of social welfare, which is costing quite enough as is.*

"We don't need the government's help, and the subsidies come with strings attached," says Tom Holt, the Oregon father of the two boys. "By signing up with the government, the provider agrees to two to four official 'visitations' from the state each year, two of them unannounced. Providers must keep attendance records and turn in menus, just in case some Agriculture Department bureaucrat wants to know what the children are eating."

In an Op-Ed piece, Holt wrote about his experience as the unwitting, unwilling, indirect recipient of a government welfare program. This irritated the local food-welfare officials.

"When the article came out, there was a large brouhaha," he recounts, "and the first thing that happened was that the bureaucrats conducted a surprise lightning inspection of the house that was baby-sitting for my kids."

How much does the government give a provider to feed two kids whose parents don't want or need the government—in a day-care center that operates for profit? And why?

I asked that of the Connecticut office of the program, which handles the free money in my part of the country.

"Well, we don't want to completely separate out the children, but we do give more money to the provider for poor children than for the rest who may not need it. The reason we pay for everyone's food is that we want to be able to supervise what the children are eating."

Really? Is checking up on kids' menus a new regulatory operation of Washington? And how much, exactly, do these peanut-butter-and-jelly inspectors provide in welfare for the unneedy?

"Those who get free lunches in school receive $1.65 for lunch in the family-child-care home," it was explained, "but others get one dollar, along with forty-seven cents more for breakfast and a snack."

That's nearly $1,000 per year per nonneedy child whose parents are suddenly on the dole. Sure, it's not a fortune, so why should parents look a federal gift horse in the mouth?

Because the money—$1.47 per day per child—comes from taxes. The parents didn't ask for it, and it only extends the seemingly endless programs designed to please politicians and bureaucrats but that extend Washington's reach into both our pocketbooks and our lives.

Is the government so hooked on giving away our money that they even have to disperse it to unwilling recipients?

3

Budget

How to Steal $6 Trillion from Social Security and Call It a "Surplus"

We hear all kinds of talk about budget "surpluses" that will keep rolling in, in virtual perpetuity. We are told there will be a multitrillion surplus up to 2013, with a whopping $685 billion surplus in just that year.

Is it true? Of course not. And where is all that money supposedly coming from?

It is a fact that the prosperity, the Wall Street boom of 1995–2000, and the large federal tax increase of 1993 did help cut down the large deficits of the early 1990s.

"The revenue that came in during those years of high Wall Street prices was 10 percent higher than usual—or an extra $150 billion a year," says a staffer on the House Budget Committee. "I don't think we can count on that going further out."

But prosperity is not the main reason the federal government—the President and the Congress, Democrats and Republicans—can make their pie-in-the-sky promises of enormous surpluses, which we hear so much about. They have marketed the concept so cleverly, and so heavily, to the nation and even to fellow politicians, that most Americans believe it. However, it is the contemporary version of the Tooth Fairy.

Would Washington actually have enough gall to invent a nonexistent surplus?

Absolutely. And unlike Lincoln's dictum, they have fooled virtually *all* of the people for all this time. As Senator Fritz Hollings of South Carolina, a maverick politician who fully understands the gimmick, says, it is a "conspiracy" designed to "loot the trust funds." It is surely the gravest and most far-reaching scam of the century.

The reality, of course, is that almost all of this largesse is the result of misappropriated Social Security money. Since this flies in the face of conventional wisdom, it surely requires a full explanation—one I hope will arm you sufficiently to disarm the Washington budget propagandists.

It is really quite simple, *if* you close your ears to the purposely complex explanations of the surplus pushers. Much of it involves the 12.4 percent FICA payroll taxes that support Social Security, but which has also created about 25 percent more money than is needed to send checks to the forty million recipients.

Those excess FICA trust funds—$156 billion in 2000—are not saved as once intended. Instead, they are immediately placed into the general fund where they are mixed with regular income tax money.

In addition, unknown to the aged, $26 billion of Medicare premiums paid in by those over 65 were put in the general fund to pay for everything from retirement of members of Congress to limos for White House staffers. By 2002 the "looted" Medicare money will reach $40 billion.

In the year 2000, Social Security FICA taxes took in $501 billion plus $65 billion in interest on the trillion-plus fund debt, for a total of $566 billion. But it only paid out $410 billion. The balance, $156 billion, was taken and spent in the

*general fund and not on the aged, widows, or disabled—one of
the great thefts of people's money in the history of the nation.*

It is all part of the "unified budget." The money, including
regular taxes and trust-fund monies, is spent every day according to the budget plan, on limos, federal pensions, tanks, welfare, what have you. The government keeps a bookkeeping
record of the money they have taken from FICA, then gives the
Social Security "trust fund" (which is just a bookkeeping entry)
a series of Treasury bonds that have an expiration date and
draw interest.

*This is how most of the fake surplus is created. It is trust-
fund money that is "borrowed" or "looted," depending on your
view, that creates the extra cash. Regular taxes plus trust-fund
money create a pool that is more than we need, which Washington, with its infinite power to confuse, calls a "budget surplus."*

And since the excess Social Security cash from an overly
large FICA tax keeps growing and growing, reaching $4 trillion
by 2013, then the fake surplus based on this money taken from
Social Security and spent in the general fund also gets larger
each year. By 2010, the misappropriated Social Security surplus
will reach $307 billion in just one year—with no known way to
redeem the debt in order to send checks to retired boomers.

Trust-fund money is a totally different kind of money.
Accounting-wise, it cannot be lumped together with the other
funds. But it is. And if you take away the Social Security trust-
fund money from the budget, as we should, almost all the "surplus" disappears.

We have two variables for the future of the mainly fake
surpluses. First, the Social Security cash the government is
expropriating, and an economy that could go sour, or at least
lose its vigor.

Come a stock market crash, or even a large slowdown, or
worse yet, a recession, and you can throw the surplus into your

fiscal wastebasket and look for ways to again dig ourselves out of a giant deficit.

So why can't we count the FICA excess and the other trust funds in our surplus figuring?

Because the gimmick is based on an Alice in Wonderland math in which the borrowed money is counted as *revenue*, which it is not. Once ordinary taxes are spent, they are gone. There is no residue, no further obligation, no loan. But that's not the case with FICA money collected for Social Security.

The government likes to think that these borrowed monies can be spent like all other taxes on whatever they want. But they can't because there are Treasury bonds left behind to compensate the fund for the borrowed cash. And these bonds cost us an extra $65 billion a year in interest—and rising.

The government euphemists like to call these bonds "assets" or "reserves," but they are no such thing. In fact, the president's budget calls them "debt securities held as assets," which is an oxymoron only Washington could concoct. *It is as if in figuring your net worth, you added your mortgage as cash!* They are government debts, plain and simple. Someday they have to be redeemed, with interest, either by me and you, or millions of young workers who will support the aged. Otherwise no one will get his promised Social Security checks.

To redeem these IOUs, we will have to raise taxes since there is not a dime of real money in the Social Security fund.

To draw a simple analogy, if a family takes out a $100,000 home-equity loan, then spends the money, was that revenue? They are left with a $100,000 note to pay off, plus interest, which puts them in debt, not in surplus. If a CEO of a public corporation borrows billions, claims it was "revenue" or "income," and thus produces a false profit, he will go to jail. Washington is doing exactly the same in claiming that there is a surplus. But in Washington's case, the crime is called "budget legislation."

So far, we have borrowed (or "looted," as Hollings says) $1.051 trillion from the Social Security account, but this sum is minuscule compared to what the government is planning to take from Social Security, up to $6 trillion by 2025, with a yearly interest cost of $350 billion!

Again, they are forgetting the debt they are leaving behind.

The mostly fake surplus is actually more dangerous than the old deficit of $250 billion. We knew what we were dealing with and could plan to bring it down. But now, as we build a "surplus" mainly on trust-fund debt, we are only fooling ourselves, and stimulating the desire for more and more spending since we supposedly can "afford" it. Cooking the books, big time, is the new extravaganza of the federal government, circa 2000 and beyond.

The root of this racket started in 1983 when the Greenspan Committee (Alan of the Federal Reserve), working with Congress, came up with a plan to *save* Social Security and guarantee the retirement of the baby boomers who would come on stream beginning in 2008 and reach a peak enrollment about 2013.

Good idea. But the problem is that when all that *extra cash* came in, politicians couldn't keep their hands off it. The Congress, Democrats up to 1994, and Republicans after that, with the cooperation of the presidents, merely took the Social Security excess funds and spent it. Every nickel. (Actually, there is presently no method for the federal government to save money. The budgets are annual, and all the money must be spent.)

When the Democrats controlled Congress, the Republicans yelled, "You're stealing the Social Security money." Then when the Republicans took over Congress in 1994 and continued to spend the FICA excess money, the Democrats yelled, "You're stealing the Social Security money."

Of course, at different times, both parties were right.

Senator Pat Moynihan of New York, considered the sage of Social Security, got up on the floor and said that what the government was doing wasn't right. We should, he said, cut back the FICA tax and go pay-as-you-go as we used to. He pointed out that we were spending the old folks' money *before* the baby boomers came to retirement age, which was the opposite of the idea behind creating a giant reserve FICA fund in the first place.

He was shouted down on both sides of the aisle.

The gimmick of using the FICA taxes under a unified budget made the deficit look much smaller than it really was, which Congress thought was just dandy. Then in 1997, all partisan debate over this scam ended when the Democrats and Republicans agreed on a Balanced Budget Amendment. Both parties suddenly had a vested interest in maintaining the fiction of a balanced budget and giant future surpluses.

Now we were told that by fiscal 1998 the country was nicely in the black. In fact, both the White House and the Congress told the people that the surplus for that year had reached $70 billion.

Was it true? Did the national debt then go down as common sense would dictate?

No.

If we can't trust the president or the Congress on fiscal matters, is there one agency in the government where you can get the truth without being taken? Yes, the place where the fiscal buck stops is the Bureau of the Public Debt, a unit of the Department of the Treasury.

The rest of the government may lie about the budget numbers and get away with it, and they regularly do. *But the Bureau of the Public Debt must be honest, otherwise the government couldn't do business with the financial markets or other nations.*

Their figures on the national debt go back to 1789 and the Constitution. The number is the cumulative deficit of government spending for all those 211 years. It is definite and inviolate and not a flimflam like our so-called surpluses.

So what does the Bureau say about 1998, for instance, when the government—both the president and the Congress—flatly announced that we had a surplus of $70 billion? Was it true? Of course not. It's the same bald-faced lie based on fake assumptions.

The Bureau is shy and unused to being quoted. But they are willing to make a simple, straightforward statement about the ledger.

I called and asked about the results for 1998. Was there indeed a $70 billion surplus?

"In 1998 we had a negative $113 billion for that year," the Bureau spokesman announced unemotionally. "The national debt went up by $113 billion, from $5.413 trillion to $5.53 trillion."

This means only one thing in any known accounting system in civilized nations: *that in 1998 we had a deficit of $113 billion.*

And what about 1999? The government claimed there was a surplus of $123 billion. Is it true?

Of course not. When the year ended, the actual result was a zero sum game with a possible minuscule surplus of $1 billion (1/2000th of the budget). The rest was borrowed Social Security money.

Meanwhile, the national debt is still going up. (See Chapter 36.)

At the end of every month, the Bureau of the Public Debt sends out a statement on the debt. You can receive it free of charge at 3:00 P.M. on the fourth workday of each month. You can ask to have it faxed, and in any event, it is immediately put on the Web at *www.publicdebt.treas.gov.*

The one for September 30, 1998, the end of that fiscal year, shows a national debt of $5,526,193,000,000.

And how large was the national debt a year later, on September 30, 1999, a year in which we supposedly had a "surplus" of $123 billion?

According to the monthly statement of the Bureau of Public Debt, the national debt had risen to $5.656 trillion, an increase of $130 billion—showing a disparity of $256 billion from the supposed, claimed, inflated, fake, cooked figures.

Some surplus.

"We have made the point over and over again that there was no real surplus in those years" says a spokesman of the Congressional Budget Office. "The government counts the money borrowed from Social Security as an asset when in reality it is a liability. It is not put aside. The people who set up the system of higher FICA taxes in the early 1980s did not realize that the government has no way to save money. Besides, there are no real trust funds. It is just an accounting device. When the time comes in 2013 when Social Security will be paying out more than it takes in, the so-called trust fund will be useless. The extra money will have to come from the Treasury."

That, of course, will mean higher taxes. Some surplus.

To understand how the government disguises the surplus, it is important to know how the national debt works. The debt is split into two parts.

The first part is marketable Treasury bonds held by investors and financial institutions. The second part of the debt is non-marketable notes held by the government, mostly for Social Security. Like the other securities, they have to be redeemed for real cash and they draw the very same interest as the debt held by outsiders.

The president says that he wants to pay down the "public" ("marketable") debt, which is fine. That's actually happening now. But what the White House doesn't say is that it is being paid down by using the trust-fund money, thus increasing the debt owed to Social Security.

As one part of the national debt—the "external" part—goes down, the other—the debt held by Social Security—goes up. Therefore, the *total* national debt continues to go up, as it did in 1998 and 1999, 2000, 2001, ad infinitum.

From the Bureau's report, we can see that the seesaw balance of taking the surplus trust-fund money to pay off one part of the debt while increasing the other is a form of Beltway trickery.

Over a period of a year, from September 30, 1998, to September 30, 1999, the debt owed to outside investors went down from $3.331 trillion to $3.232 trillion, a reduction of $99 billion. *But meanwhile, the debt held by the government went up to $129 billion, an even larger amount.*

There's nothing like having two sets of books, which is what the government does. One is called the "budget," with its fake giant surpluses and gimmickry of a "unified" accounting. The other is a reconciliation of the national debt, which is the only tally that expresses the reality.

Is everyone blind to the scam? I am not alone, even if I sometimes think so.

Tom Schatz, president of Citizens Against Government Waste, tries to clarify the budget fantasy. "Before anyone runs off to spend the 'surplus,'" he explains, "it is imperative to understand how the books are being cooked in Washington and the consequences of deciding whether to spend or save the 'extra' money."

Not long ago the Concord Coalition ran a full-page advertisement in the *New York Times* to try to educate the public and burst Washington's fantasy surpluses. It was signed by two former senators, Warren Rudman (R, NH) and Sam Nunn (D., GA), along with Peter G. Peterson, former secretary of commerce. The prestigious trio tried to explain it all to the uninitiated:

"The official budget balance includes Social Security's current trust fund surplus. Senator Moynihan reminds us that this surplus is supposed to be saved to prefund the Baby Boomers' retirement—and denounces double counting it as 'thievery.'"

These appeals to reason flew by like a winter wind, apparently misunderstood, or disregarded, while members of Congress and government employees who understood the gimmick were afraid to blow the whistle. Only Speaker-never-to-be Bob Livingston, before he resigned from Congress, let the cat out of the fiscal bag a bit. He said that as Speaker, he would try to create a *real* surplus without taking advantage of the Social Security money.

Senator Moynihan of New York is one of those who knows the inner workings of the system. A spokesman for the senator states that he didn't appreciate the Concord Coalition quoting him as saying the scam was "thievery."

But, says the spokesman, "the senator knows exactly what's going on and is trying to stop it through legislation. He and Senator Robert Kerrey of Nebraska have put in a bill, Senate S-21, that would break the unified budget and have Social Security stand alone, separate from the present commingling with other federal funds. Then the government wouldn't be able to take the FICA excess funds and spend them as they're doing now."

The bill would *lower* the payroll (FICA) tax from the present 12.4 percent for employee and employer to 10.4 percent, placing Social Security on a pay-as-you-go basis, as it was before 1983, but with slightly lower benefits.

Voilà. Should the bill be passed, that would be the end of the giant "surplus" talk, present or future. We'd have a return to truth in budgeting, obviously a painful exercise for our politicians.

In this whole maelstrom, one person of authority does stand out as a profile in courage. That, as I have mentioned, is Senator Ernest F. ("Fritz") Hollings, the white-haired veteran from South Carolina. He has been on a rampage about the fake surplus and the use of our trust funds to patch up the budget.

"In reality," he writes, "the deficit is merely moved from

the general fund into the Social Security trust fund," a technique he openly calls "a fraud." He points out that the original Greenspan reform in 1983 recommended that Social Security be removed from the unified budget to protect it from being looted.

"I struggled to institute this recommendation," he writes. "Congress overwhelmingly approved and President Bush signed into law (on November 5, 1990) Section 13301 of the Budget Act forbidding the president or Congress from reporting a budget using Social Security trust funds. This structure is violated every day."

He has produced a chart showing what most of the so-called surplus is based on. It shows that we have taken over a trillion from Social Security by 2000, which will rise to $2.74 trillion by 2008 when the boomers will start retiring, and much more by 2013.

In addition, we should not forget that all these extra trillions in trust-fund debt add billions in interest to our real budget, a punishing and unexpected side effect of the surplus scam.

"We should have $3.2 trillion reserve when payments to retiring baby boomers will start to exceed revenues," Hollings writes. "But because we will have already spent the money for other things, we will have to raise taxes or cut benefits to pay Social Security recipients." (Though citizens are generally ignorant of the scam, many young people are intuitively—and correctly—skeptical of the system.)

Their skepticism is verified by the prestigious Concord Coalition. In a full-page ad in the *New York Times* of October 1, 2000 they point out that:

1. Social Security, Medicare, and Medicaid will take 81 percent of the budget by 2040.
2. Social Security will have a $500 billion annual dollar deficit by 2027.

3. Social Security will take almost 18 percent of payrolls by 2040, a 75 percent hike.

4. Under the current system, a twenty-five-year-old will get only 72 percent of current benefits.

Much of this is due to the missing $4 trillion of FICA money spent in the general fund by 2013 to make it look as if there are giant surpluses.

That plus the simple fact that soon there will be only two workers supporting one retiree.

It doesn't add up despite political doubletalk about "lock-boxes." It is merely obfuscation meant to dealy the inevitable—privatizing, lower benefits, or much higher FICA taxes.

This looting of the fund, and replacing cash that has been spent with paper IOUs, is one of the most despicable acts of government in this or any century. Masquerading it as a surplus only compounds the crime. And the idea that adding still more paper to the Social Security trust fund will "save it," as many, including the president, propose, is a macabre joke.

As Hollings says: "For everyone crying 'Save Social Security,' the first order of business is to stop destroying it by looting the fund."

Amen.

So much for federal budgeting in the new millennium.

Unless we correct this double counting, double record keeping, cooked books, spending trust fund cash and replacing it with trillions of Social Security paper that has to be redeemed by us or our children, the "unified" government budget will continue to be what it has become: an uncivilized, false, destructive record of what it takes to run our government.

C

4

Computers

WANTED: Teenage Hackers

An audit by the General Services Administration, which does the equipping and housekeeping for many government agencies, turned up what may shock us, but which was no surprise to Washington insiders.

It seems that the GSA spent $121 million on a computer system to monitor building needs, only to have to eventually cancel the project. The reason? "Ineffective oversight," a federal euphemism for not knowing what in the heck they were doing in the first place.

If there is a champion in Washington's multibillion-dollar waste race, it is surely the purchase and use of computer systems, a subject about which the federal government is almost as ignorant as a puzzled father watching his fourteen-year-old son debug Windows 2000 for him.

Speaking of the misuse and inefficiency of the multibillion-dollar computer systems at the Department of Defense, the IRS, and the FAA, the acting comptroller general of the U.S. offers a discouraging word:

"These efforts are having serious trouble meeting cost, schedule, and/or performance goals. Such problems are all too common in federal automation projects. Agencies have obligated over $145 billion during the past six years building, buying, and maintaining computer systems and networks. Yet this vast investment has yielded poor returns."

That's a real understatement.

Former senator William S. Cohen (later secretary of defense) pulled together a set of horror stories about the waste and ignorance of Washington in the computer field. Entitled "Computer Chaos: Billions Wasted Buying Federal Computer Systems," the report points out that Washington spends $25 billion a year on computers—over 5 percent of the entire discretionary budget. Yet it is far from getting its money's worth.

He lists the following federal goofs:

- The Federal Aviation Administration (FAA) computer technology is so old (and failing) that they had to buy vintage vacuum tubes from Poland and search Radio Shack and junkyards for spare parts to keep the system running. The FAA relies on 1960s mainframe computers that are as large as a truck but are only one-tenth as powerful as a personal computer.

- The FAA's computer modernization of its air traffic control is "plagued by poor management and billions in cost overruns and recently restructured after a ten year modernization effort came to naught."

- At the IRS, they are in the midst of their "third unsuccessful attempt" since 1968 to modernize its computers. Says the report: "Outdated IRS computer systems have contributed to a $70 billion

> backlog in uncollected taxes and unreliable financial records which even the General Accounting Office could not adequately audit."

Deputy Treasury secretary Lawrence Summers (now Treasury Secretary) later testified before a congressional committee, confessing that its $20 billion IRS computer modernization program was "badly off the track." As a result, he says, many IRS computers cannot "talk" to each other. *Instead, cumbersome magnetic tapes are frequently flown around the country because the information cannot be transmitted electronically!*

- The Farmers Home Administration (now the Farm Service Agency) managed its loan portfolio manually by using color-coded index cards, having spent $200 million unsuccessfully on computer systems to do the job.

- Using a host of "archaic computer systems," the Department of Defense operates 161 different accounting systems, making it difficult, if not impossible, to audit defense expenditures.

In another report, the GAO said Defense "squandered" almost $16 million on unjustified computer purchases. One contractor was loaned $1 million of computer equipment, but less than $750,000 of it was found in a later inventory. Another contractor was awarded $2 million to develop a computer system, which was found to be so flawed as to be useless. More than $8 million was spent on three hundred computer work stations that were neither needed nor formally requested.

The mayhem is continuous and pervasive. At the National Weather Service, a $618 million Advanced Weather Interactive

Processing System (AWIPS) has segments that are incompatible with each other. Worse yet, its software is often written in several different computer languages.

In purchasing new systems, the government is often grandiose, buying equipment they cannot manage. As one critic pointed out, they do not presently have the "intellectual capital" to do the computer job necessary. And the government acts very slowly in the fast-moving computer technology world. Because of Washington's complex, lengthy buying procedures, the chances are good that the technology will be obsolete by the time it's delivered.

Almost every federal agency seems involved in the Washington computer chaos.

- Because of unreliable computer-generated information, the Department of Agriculture's multibillion-dollar funds are at risk of being lost or spent the wrong way.

- The Department of Defense's computer operation is so primitive and distorted that they have identified $41 *billion* in payments they cannot match up with invoices!

- The Department of Housing and Urban Development lacks effective computer control over $100 billion in contracts and cannot learn if money is going to eligible recipients. Their seventy-five different computer systems have only minimal or nonexistent ability to "talk" to each other and share information.

- Because of computer inadequacy and incompetence, the Department of Education cannot produce reliable financial reports on over $60 billion of outstanding loans and $31 billion in yearly expenditures, loans, and grants. As one result, millions of dollars of unauthorized student loans have been made.

- The Department of Veterans Affairs operates 150 different computer systems, many of which are incompatible.

To try to correct the federal computer chaos, the Congress passed the 1996 Clinger-Cohen Act, formally named the "Information Technology Management Reform Act." In late fall of 1997, the House Committee on Government Reform and Oversight held hearings on its implementation.

The bill hoped to ensure that federal monies spent on information technology—mainly computers—was used wisely. It set up the new post of chief information officer in each of the cabinet offices and major agencies, twenty-four in all. The goal, says the committee report, is "the development of an effective and an efficient, mission-oriented, user-oriented, results-oriented information technology practice in each and every federal agency."

From their lips to God's ear.

Having a chief information officer in every agency is a good idea, but what has happened to date? Very little. They have appointed twenty-four CIOs. And?

"I'm sorry to say," confides a staff member and technical expert at the House Subcommittee on Government Management, Information, and Technology, "that the bill was well intentioned when it set up the CIO system. But of the twenty-four chief information officers appointed, I'm afraid most are not qualified."

He outlines the four criteria for a CIO who could take the government out of its present computer chaos:

1. That he be a full-time information employee. Unfortunately, about ten of the twenty-four have two—or even three—jobs. Most of these double as chief financial officer and chief information officer, which makes it virtually impossible to do a good job. Each job requires different skills and attitudes.

2. That he know something about the agency and hasn't just been transferred from, say, Agriculture to Defense.

3. That he have an information technology background.

4. That the technical people report to him, not someone else. The Clinger-Cohen Act did not specify that, and most technical people still do not report to the CIO.

"Overall, I'd say that only four of the twenty-four new CIOs are qualified for the job," says the House staffer. "Naturally little progress has been made in solving our computer problems."

He points out that the "IRS Modernization Blueprint," created to bring their computer up to snuff, has gone nowhere.

"Firstly, the Y2K [the year 2000] problem took all their energies," he points out. "And secondly, the recently appointed head of the IRS, who happens to be a technical man, looked at their blueprint and said it was 'god-awful.' It had to be redesigned and they have made no substantial progress on modernization."

The only part of the Clinger-Cohen bill that has helped a little is the procurement of off-the-shelf items like personal computers, which are now more easily purchased at decent prices.

"But that doesn't help the big mainframe problems—the giant systems still being used by the government that are antiquated and don't talk to each other," the House staff member explained. "We've made virtually no progress in that direction. Reform is still years ahead. Who knows how many years? There has been no substantial improvement in the large federal computer systems. We're still working with dinosaurs."

So what is the answer? There are a few:

1. Amend the Clinger-Cohen Act to require that *all* twenty-four CIOs are masters at computer technology and hold only one job.

2. Have these new appointees design modern systems and have them replace all the old incompatible ones. In the long run, it will be the cheapest money spent.

3. And this might be the best solution. The political appointees in Washington should visit my alma mater, Stuyvesant High School, the scientific scholarship school in Manhattan that walks away with so many Intel (formerly Westinghouse) prizes. Organize a group of teenage computer whizzes and give them a consulting contract to fix the whole rotten government computer operation.

It'll cost peanuts, and I guarantee you that Washington's computers will finally work—for the first time.

5

Conventions, Presidential

They're Partying on Our Nickel

Remember the good time that all the delegates, the alternate delegates, their wives, girlfriends, boyfriends, hangers-on, and the media had at Houston and New York in 1996 at the national presidential conventions of the Republican and Democratic parties? And an equal celebration of the pols in Philadelphia and Los Angeles in the summer of 2000?

We watched it on television and smiled at the shenanigans, the overdecorated settings, the music, the banners and bunting, the stanchions, glitz, funny hats, and buttons galore.

What we didn't see on television were all the private parties, luncheons, dinners, and evening receptions where the catered food and the liquor—from caviar to Chivas Regal—flowed like the Nile and people danced the night away.

We shrugged. Maybe some of us were jealous of the good time being had by all. (Years ago I was alternate delegate at one of them, and it is fun.) But why should we care how much they throw away? It's their money—isn't it?

Unfortunately, it's not. You and I were actually there, at

least in spirit. You might not know it, but you—the voter—picked up the *basic* tab for the two presidential nominating convention blowouts in 2000. Whether you liked it or not.

You see, these quadrennial presidential confabs are paid for by the federal government—partying, liquor, hors d'oeuvres and all.

In 1992 each political party received a check from the government for over $11 million to throw their convention. In 1996 it had gone up to $12 million. For the summer of 2000, each party received $13 million, or a total of $26 million.

Did you say that our money even covers music, food, and liquor? That doesn't sound kosher.

Well, host groups, quasimunicipal organizations, can raise extra money for the fun time, generally from corporate sponsors, but Washington is legally responsible for virtually any cost, including celebrating.

To check out this illogical concept, I called the Federal Elections Commission (FEC), which handles the payouts. They weren't sure themselves, but they researched it. They said, yes, the delegates can booze it up on the federal nickel. They even sent me the regulations—9008.7 and 9008.8.

The regulations first explain the usual expenses for "preparing, maintaining, and dismantling the physical site of the convention, including rental of the hall, platforms and seating, decorations, telephone, security, convention hall utilities and other related costs." Then it goes on to state that the federal money also covers:

"Official party convention activities, including but not limited to dinners, concerts, and receptions, where such activities are paid for with public money."

Says the FEC spokesman, citing the word *receptions:* "Yes, that includes food and liquor." He didn't remember any such highbrow events as "concerts."

Can the political parties afford to pick up the tab?

Anyone familiar with the "soft money" racket of American politics knows that's a silly question, and then some. The FEC says that in the most recent two-year cycle, the parties, in both "hard" and "soft" contributions, took in almost $700 million. The Republican take was $416,513,249, while the Democrats weren't too far behind with over $250 million. In the four-year period, together they took in almost $1.5 billion!

Can they afford $26 million for their conventions? I would say so.

In many ways, the conventions are becoming obsolete. They are painfully predictable now that most of the delegates are chosen in the state primaries, beginning with New Hampshire. The "front-runner" is almost always chosen on the first ballot as the presidential nominee. Without the drama of backroom bargaining and deal making, the television viewership is much lower, and dropping each four years.

I really don't mind if the political parties continue the ritual of their presidential conventions, antique though they are becoming.

But I tell you this, and you can pass it on to your congressman: *We should change the law immediately so that beginning now, we won't be spending another nickel on this obviously partisan, and increasingly boring, activity.*

And besides, this business of politicians living it up on my nickel—without me there to enjoy it—has got to stop.

6

Corporate Welfare

You Mean I'm Subsidizing Intel?

In affluent Silicon Valley, an ingenious inventor and entrepreneur named Alex Balkanski was, until recently, CEO of C-Cube Microsystems, Inc., a high-tech firm that compresses video signals. They make it possible to put ten digital channels, instead of a single analog one, on one satellite transponder.

A venture-capital-funded company, they lost money for years while their shareholders waited patiently for the technology to take off, and pay off, which it finally did. They became a leader in their field and even won an Emmy for their contribution to television.

"But then shortly after C-Cube started making a profit," relates T. J. Rodgers, himself a Silicon Valley entrepreneur and a member of C-Cube's board, "we were shocked to find out that the U.S. government had funded one of our competitors."

Rodgers says he is angry that Washington was unfairly competing with private industry and hurting the company's chances of success.

What the government did with one of its ubiquitous subsidy programs to private industry was give a Department of Commerce ATP (Advanced Technology Program) grant to a much larger company—LSI Logic Corporation, a billion-dollar, top-ten semiconductor company—to help fund their work in the same field of video compression.

Uncle Sam was playing the failed Japanese game, trying to stage-manage capitalism and pick winners and losers, helping some and hurting others, an activity I don't recall reading about in the Constitution.

The U.S. government calls it "government-business partnerships," a typical hyped Washington phrase to cover their meddling—with our cash—in hundreds of American businesses.

But a wide variety of Americans, conservatives such as CATO and The Heritage Foundation, and liberals such as Ralph Nader and the Progressive Policy Institute, and nonpartisan operations such as Citizens Against Government Waste, call it what it is—corporate welfare, an egregious waste of the taxpayer's hard-earned money.

Corporate welfare is a system of government subsidies to the titans of industry, who ingeniously take an estimated $75 billion a year out of the public treasury with results no less wasteful than the ignorant, duplicate government welfare programs for individuals and families (see Chapter 34, Welfare).

Back at Silicon Valley, the government went into still another large business, Sematech, which was formed to do cooperative research among high-tech companies so we could better compete against Japan. Sounds like a good idea, but they weren't subsidizing small start-ups with more science than cash.

Instead, $800 million of taxpayer money and an exemption

from the antitrust law have gone into a handful of *giant* electronic companies that make that much money in profit each month. And they don't have to pay the money back after the people's investment brings profits on-line.

The list of welfare beneficiaries in Silicon Valley and elsewhere includes such "needy" firms as:

- **Intel**
- **Motorola**
- **Digital Equipment (now part of Compaq)**
- **IBM**
- **AT&T**
- **Texas Instruments**
- **Advanced Micro Devices**
- **Rockwell**
- **National Semiconductor**

These are only a few of the recipients of taxpayer largesse. Other corporate subsidies, like the Advanced Technology Program, go to such firms as United Airlines, Xerox, DuPont, Caterpillar, TRW, Eastman Kodak, General Motors, and Shell Petroleum.

The system is simple: The taxpayers take the risk that new technologies will emerge. The corporations get the profit.

Even in that unequal battle, the firms often take advantage of the powerless taxpayer. A General Accounting Office report on ATP showed that in many cases, the "overhead" paid by Uncle Sam exceeds the money spent on research!

They also found that 65 percent of the recipients of taxpayer cash didn't even attempt to secure private funding for taxpayer subsidies. Says Congressman Ed Royce (R., CA), who has put in legislation to close down ATP: "We must keep in mind that what we are discussing here is the redistribution of wealth from hardworking American families to large multimillion-dollar concerns . . ."

He points out that ATP, which is supposedly a catalyst for high-tech R & D, drains the treasury of $203 million a year, but is small change compared to the $51 *billion* invested by private industry.

There are 125 corporate welfare programs emanating from virtually every cabinet agency—especially Commerce and Agriculture—that *give* our money to private companies. One of the most annoying (it still bothers me to think about it) is the Market Access Program (MAP), once called the Market Promotion Program and exposed in my 1992 volume, but which still flourishes.

In this racket, *we*—and not the companies—pay to advertise famous brand-name food products in overseas newspapers and magazines so that their bottom line will grow as our pockets shrink.

The program is expensive. Over the last ten years, the Department of Agriculture has transferred over a billion dollars to such giant MAP welfare beneficiaries as Gallo wines, which has a $3.5 billion annual gross. Tyson Foods received $500,000 in tax money for overseas promotion; $730,000 went to Welch's; $308,000 to Ocean Spray; $526,000 for the Pillsbury Company; and $281,000 to the penurious Campbell Soup Co. Even the Kentucky Distillers Association, which passes on the subsidies to brand-name liquors, picked up $1 million from Uncle Sam.

The handouts are even going to pet-food companies to lure dogs and cats worldwide. The Petfood Institute shared $420,000, and Ralston Purina, a multibillion-dollar maker of gourmet pet food, wasn't beneath picking up $239,000. Even candy maker M & M Mars received $1 million in sugary government deals not long ago.

There is something unethical, even devilish, about Congress giving away our money to corporate giants. But knowing the obfuscating Beltway mentality, it is probably understandable since these same companies are large contributors to both parties, and their paid lobbyists on K Street move effortlessly about in the halls of Congress and committee rooms, where the average citizen is absent or unknown.

One area of corporate welfare that should gall taxpayers is the underwriting of business loans by Uncle Sam. This is not the Small Business Administration, which has its own problems (see Chapter 28, Small-Business Criminals) and a giant default rate on its $10 billion-a-year loans. This is something that should be called the "Big-Business Administration."

One program that feeds these giants is the Export-Import Bank, which is an ingenious business dodge invented by Congress. The scam here is simple. Large firms sell products overseas, whether airplanes or business machines, in the *hope* that the customer will pay, or that the developing country won't go belly-up financially. If they do default, Ex-Im Bank, or another federal agency, the Overseas Private Investment Corporation (OPIC), will pick up the tab, which can run into billions.

A big borrower of money directly from Uncle Sam, or with loans guaranteed by the Ex-Im Bank, for example, is Boeing, whose sales are worldwide. In effect, we're subsidizing them by backstopping defaults if small foreign airlines don't pay up. The Ex-Im Bank, which has an annual appropriation of $772 million, has already lost $8 billion in its operations, most in the last fifteen years, plus new subsidy costs of some $800 million a year.

Some bank.

The other "bank," OPIC, underwrites lower-interest loans and insures many companies, including Coca-Cola, against political instability overseas as they invest in unstable developing countries, increasing their worldwide operations at the taxpayer's risk—not theirs. OPIC has overseas liabilities of some $20 billion. Says *Barrons* magazine about the operation: "It has been dishing out sweet deals to wealthy patrons of both major parties . . . providing them with terms to die for."

General Motors, which is reputed to have $20 billion in cash, is also the recipient of corporate welfare, as are Chrysler and Ford, both worldwide giants. With this program, which has the tantalizing title "Partnership for a New Generation of Vehicles," we give $240 million a year to the Big Three to do research—as if they can't afford it. When they do come up with new vehicles (meanwhile Toyota already has a mixed electric-gas car on the market), they will not pay back the $1 billion invested, nor will they share the profits with taxpayers.

The list of corporate welfare—in the form of direct cash subsidies, grants, loans, or tax loopholes—is long, and the rules are complex.

The programs also include:

- **Fossil Energy Research and Development**, which so far has spent $1.5 billion to develop new technology for oil, coal, and natural gas, an activity the corporations involved should pay for.

- **Ethanol, or gasahol.** Research on this, which is intended to find a mixed gasoline-alcohol fuel for cars, has cost us almost a billion dollars thus far, mainly to support giant agribusiness firms. Tax breaks for producers of the fuel will cost us another $1.8 billion over seven years.

- Clean Coal Technology, a half-billion-dollar program, subsidizes large corporations who try to lower coal emissions.

- General Agreement to Borrow. Part of the International Monetary Fund—a potential $3.5 billion package to bail out countries in economic distress.

In addition, there are several corporate welfare programs that I first exposed in 1992, but which I will revisit in Part Two, a look at what's happened to a dozen or more boondoggles since then. The corporate welfare roster there includes Rural Utilities Services (once the REA); timber road building by the Forest Service for wood products companies; subsidized "Essential Air" to provide discount air service to select communities; government power plants that sell discount electricity with taxpayer money.

Some of these programs are complex, but one thing is simple and clear. Whoever came up with the cockamamie idea of taxpayers supporting private businesses had not studied the constitutional purposes of democratic capitalism.

What is the solution to this enormous scam?

Simple. Congress should pass my "Antisubsidy" bill, which would make it illegal for the federal government to give any grants or loans, no matter how small or large, to any private business in America.

This will wipe out corporate welfare once and for all, and it will also instantly eliminate more billions spent in the name of Washington favoritism.

The savings will be at least $75 billion a year, which translates into almost a 10 percent cut in all taxes paid by people filing the Form 1040 to the Internal Revenue Service.

Until then, Mr. and Ms. Members of Congress, and presidents in the White House, I have one minor request. I'm thinking of starting a unique little Internet company for nonfiction writers in my garage. Whom do I see in Washington to get a small—maybe $25 million—start-up grant for superadvanced technology?

D

7

Demonstration Projects

Highways to Pork Heaven

In 1991, to great outcry from waste-watchers, Congress passed what was called ISTEA, or Iced Tea—the Intermodal Surface Transportation Efficiency Act—a massive $153 billion highway bill.

Not that people don't want highways, but attached to the bill were what are euphemistically called "demonstration projects." These were not regular roads requested by the state highway commissions, but special requests that, in the vernacular, were wonderful examples of highway *pork*, several of them gimmicks only tangentially related to roads.

In a way, they "demonstrated" to local voters that their member of Congress was determined to bring home budget-busting goodies even if they weren't needed. One was a $35 million monorail for Altoona, a town in Pennsylvania with a population of 57,000. Although the project was finally killed after public outrage, it's no coincidence that Altoona is in the district of Representative Bud Shuster, now chairman of the

Committee on Transportation and Infrastructure, the man who makes and breaks roads nationwide.

(Shuster actually has a highway named after him.)

After 460 "demo" projects that cost taxpayers $6.8 billion in 1991, some congressmen swore "never again." They would no longer support highway pork. Once the penny-pinching Republicans took Congress, most were sure they would end billions in useless demonstrations.

There was a precedent for that hope. In 1987 President Ronald Reagan, when faced with a highway bill with 152 demonstration projects costing $1.8 billion, quickly vetoed the bill. Then in 1994, the Republicans took both houses of Congress, and repeated the coup in 1996. But did that end highway demo projects?

Hardly. In fact, it has *grown* beyond the expectations of the hungriest of members, proving that the pigs eat happily on both sides of the trough.

In the bipartisan Balanced Budget Act of 1997, they agreed on spending $184 billion on highways, which was about the inflation-adjusted equal to the 1991 authorization. But that wasn't enough for Congressman Shuster. The chairman boosted the stake, and by the time committee members and friends, political and otherwise, had put in their bids, the cost of the new highway bill—passed in 1998 and signed by the president—was a record-smashing $218 billion!

House Budget Committee Chairman John Kasich (R., OH), an opponent of the Shuster bill, says it has exceeded the balanced budget caps by $26 billion.

Demonstration projects are a relatively new gimmick of professional porkers. The 1982 transportation bill had only ten projects at a cost of $365 million. But the number of demos has skyrocketed in recent years. By 1991 it had jumped to 460, and then exploded to *1,850* projects in 1998, along with a rise in price from $6.8 billion to $9.3 billion.

Called "TEA-21," an advertising acronym for "Transportation Equity Act for the Twenty-First Century," the newest highway bill includes a vast number of unneeded projects from coast to coast. Many have little, if anything, to do with a better highway system.

They include:

- $12 million for an Appalachian Transportation Institute at Marshall University in West Virginia.

- $12 million for a Dwight David Eisenhower Transportation Fellowship Program.

- $3 million for a documentary film about highway infrastructure, which may well star Congressman Shuster.

- $500,000 to study better access to the Kennedy Center in Washington, D.C.

- $1.5 million to study parking at truck stops (perhaps including better access to Joe's Eatery).

- $9 million, much of it for the construction of the National Scenic Byways Center (a Greyhound Bus history display) in Duluth, Minnesota.

- $12.4 million for the Secretary of the Interior for a new visitors' center in West Virginia for the Federal Lands Highway Program. Perhaps they forgot that there are already five existing national parks visitors' centers within twenty-five miles of the new one.

- $6 million for the Independence Gateway Transportation Center in Philadelphia.

- $1.6 million for an intermodal transportation center at the Missouri Botanical Garden, a curious mixture of interests.

- $10 million for a Geographical Information System in Washington, D.C.

- $20 million for the Mon-Fayette Expressway in Pennsylvania.

- $10 million for a bicycle and pedestrian walkway from Union Station in Washington, D.C, to Silver Spring, Maryland, another amenity for the pampered federal district.

- $4 million for the enhancement of an intermodal facility in Philadelphia, including purchase of passenger vans for reverse commuting of visitors.

- $1.2 million for a Washington (State) Pass visitor facility.

- $4 million for a parking lot at the Peoria (Illinois) City River Center.

- $3.8 million for a parking lot and pedestrian bridge in Yorba Linda, California.

- $4.4 million for the "beautification" of Route A1A in Daytona, Florida, in the districts of two members of the Transportation Committee, one Democrat and one Republican, a case of creative bipartisanship in how to spend our money.

- $2.7 million to enhance the Maple Avenue streetscape in Vienna, Virginia.

- $3.5 million to rehabilitate a "historic" train depot in San Bernardino, California.

- **$2.5 million to renovate the Harrisburg Transportation Center in Pennsylvania, the favorite state of Congressman Shuster.**

- **$445,000 for a Hudson River scenic overlook from Route 9 to the waterfront in Poughkeepsie, New York.**

Sometimes the projects are so blatantly wasteful that congresspeople have to fudge a little to even get it through committee. One $7 million demo claims that the money is for "transportation enhancement activities within the Lehigh Landing Area of the Delaware and Lehigh Canal National Heritage Corridor."

Sounds impressive. But an Associated Press reporter learned that the money is really scheduled for local recreation—to build still another automobile museum, a picnic pavilion, baseball and soccer fields, and most important, a boathouse for Lehigh University's sculling crew.

It's rather obvious what this "demonstrates."

One forgotten part of the whole highway fight is that the present method of naming actual roads to be financed out of the federal treasury is in violation of a House regulation. In 1914 the House adopted a rule that spelled it out: "It shall not be in order for any bill providing general legislation in relation to roads to contain any provision for any specific road."

The sage old-timers feared that it would set up a stampede for highway pork, and they have been proven absolutely right.

The startling aspect of demo projects is that their sponsors are often hawks about saving in other areas. But when it comes to hometown highway pork, their thought processes go awry.

In fact, the states involved usually don't want these projects, but they are overruled by a manic Congress.

"All roads, you know, are state and local, even if they have a U.S. label, like U.S. 1," explains a federal auditor who handles highways. "But in deciding how highway money should be spent, the Federal Highway Administration and the states consult, using specific guidelines. But when members of Congress want highway projects for their own districts, they just earmark them right in the law and it goes over the top. There's no screening and they don't have to meet state criteria."

What happens is that money goes to projects favored by members of Congress *instead* of those projects that states believe have a high priority for a better infrastructure.

In a game of cynical gamesmanship, nontransportation members of Congress have less of a chance to bring home the highway bacon. An analysis of demo pork by *Roll Call*, a newspaper that covers Congress, showed that Congressman Shuster used the bill to punish his enemies and reward his committee members and political friends.

"If you were on the committee, you got about $40 million, and if not, about $15 million," said Rep. David Hobson (R., OH). "If you opposed Shuster, you got less." In addition, Republican members of the seventy-three-member committee got bonuses based on their seniority.

But Shuster also extracted bipartisan vengeance. While two friendly Republican committee members got $75 million each for their hometowns, Rep. Chip Pickering (R., MS)—one of only three committee Republicans to oppose Shuster's bill—was cut down to only $35 million.

The money for all this congressional conniving comes from our federal gas taxes, which were once only a few pennies. They were raised to 9 cents a gallon in the 1980s, then to 14 cents in the budget deal of 1990, then later on to 18.4 cents, the present tax. This, of course, is on top of the state gas taxes, which range from 9 cents in New Jersey to 32 cents in Connecticut.

The cash goes into the Highway Trust Fund, where it has been regularly abused by the government. For many years it was raided, with almost a third of it funneled into the general account for anything from congressmen's salaries to limousines. At the same time, the remaining money was "borrowed" by the government in order to mask the deficit.

Then in 1998, the gas tax was left alone so that it could finance the giant TEA-21 bill. But the government had to cheat, at least a little. The Highway Trust Fund has always been paid interest from the Treasury, like any other part of the national debt.

Now, at the urging of porker Shuster, the leadership in Congress agreed that the unused gas-tax money will no longer receive any interest. Why? So that we can build still more transportation centers and parking lots.

Who, we may ask, decided that Washington could use federal tax money to build local bike paths, like $1.2 million for the extension of one in Saint Louis, or improve drainage on a local street, like Sixth Street in Menominee, Michigan? Whatever happened to the local autonomy and function of the thousands of towns in America?

The answer is that, like much in American life, they are suddenly "federalized" when they become objects of the Washington pork lust.

Some members of Congress still have their wits about them. In May 1998, after final approval of H.R. 2400—the TEA-21 bill—Senator John McCain of Arizona wrote a letter to President Clinton asking him to line-item veto (that power then existed) the $9 billion of "whimsical" demonstration projects that were "locality specific, low priority, unnecessary and wasteful spending."

Of course, he lost.
What to do? Simple.

1. Both houses need to pass an amendment that requires states to certify that their federal highway money is being used only for "priority" roads. If not, no gas-tax money can be spent on the project. This will eliminate almost all "demo" projects.

2. Once the federal 18.4-cents-per-gallon gas tax is collected by Washington, we should simply hand it back to the states in grants with no strings attached. Then they can build the roads *they want* without federal political greed.

In the process, we'll be saving at least $10 billion.

E

8

Earned Income Tax Credit (EITC)

Are You Getting Your
Free Money from Uncle Sam?

It's not earned.

It's not real income.

It's not a tax.

Then what is it?

EITC is *free money* that often comes in the form of an annual check from the IRS.

Is this a tax refund? No, a refund is when Uncle Sam pays back the money you overpaid in withholding—but without the interest, which the government, in its inimitable way, has kept.

No, EITC is a reward for taxes you never paid or never owed. It comes in the form of a credit or a check from the IRS and the Department of the Treasury. It's not just a one-time gift from the taxpayers, but a *perpetual* yearly check, one of the strangest, and often one of the most fraudulent and expensive, operations in the Washington bag of programs.

Since it's an eccentric program, is it small and inconsequential?

Hardly. *Over twenty million Americans are on this dole, and they take more than $28 billion from the U.S. Treasury each year.*

Is it welfare? Is this only for people who sit home and collect checks mainly because they have children and are unmarried?

Absolutely not. This has nothing to do with regular welfare programs. This free money is for working people who the government believes don't make enough to live on nicely. Does that mean that they make only $10,000 a year—which is about the minimum wage for forty hours a week?

No, EITC is truly generous with taxpayers' money. It doesn't only give away money to the poor—a family of four who by definition makes almost $17,000. Most of the EITC beneficiaries are well above the poverty level.

In fact (and this astounded me), you can get your free money even if you earn considerably more than the average American. Although the typical American paycheck for full-time workers is about $29,000, the limit for EITC eligibility is now $30,095.

Equally important, there is no wealth test for this free green. You can be worth millions, you can own a mansion and a yacht, but if you didn't earn more than $30,095 this year and didn't receive more than $2,250 in investment income, the EITC is there to support you with our tax money.

What's the catch? There really is none. *Free money is free money.* Especially when it comes from Saint Washington, the patron saint of freebies. The unfortunate reality is that Washington has set up a system whereby one neighbor, through the IRS, sends a check to his neighbor who may earn a few dollars less than he.

Does it mean, though, that no one gets more than a couple of hundred dollars from EITC? Just enough to smooth out the rough edges?

No. Quite the opposite. The program, which started in 1975 to repay low-income workers for part of their regressive Social Security tax, has grown out of proportion and has been expanding faster than any federal giveaway. In 1990 the maximum you could collect was $953. By 1993 it had risen to $1,511. By 1994 it was $2,528. By 1997 it had lofted to $3,656, then to $3,756, and headed upward to $4,000 a year.

As part of the program's tattered history, it even sent out checks without people asking for them. In 1992, as an "experiment" in largesse, the IRS sent out $400 million to those EITC recipients who *seemed* entitled to them. The tragic part is that $175 million of the payments were later considered to be in error.

So who gets the money today? Let's say you are self-employed, have two children, and made $12,000 net after all expenses. Just look up the IRS table, file your taxes, and put in a claim for EITC free money. They'll either take a handsome sum of $3,756 off your taxes, or in many cases, merely send you a Treasury check for that amount.

Marvin Kosters of the American Enterprise Institute states that almost 90 percent of EITC recipients pay no federal taxes, so most of the money comes in the mail as a cash bonus, a new form of welfare. The odds on this are considerably better than getting a sweepstakes check from Ed McMahon.

What if you are closer to the average American and made $22,500 and have two children? You'll also get a nice check or credit for almost $1,500.

What if you're seventy, and still work and earn $5,500 a year part-time, but you also get $1,500 a month from Social Security, or $18,000 a year? You have a total of $23,500 in income. And, I forgot, own your own house free and clear and have a portfolio of Microsoft stock worth $100,000. You wouldn't expect free green from Uncle Sam, would you?

Well, you're wrong. The reason is that Social Security is not counted as income in EITC figuring, nor is your wealth. Get out your pencil and pad and write this down if you fit the preceding model. When you file your next Form 1040, apply for EITC, because you're entitled to either credit (not just a deduction) or a check for $341 from the IRS.

And what if you're a retired millionaire but work part-time at a drugstore just to keep active? You'll get your EITC money, which you can add to your millions.

One ludicrous benefit of the program is that, unlike other taxpayers who have money *taken out* of their paycheck each payday, an EITC recipient can have his yearly dole distributed in parts, and *added* each month to his paycheck.

The EITC program is totally distorted geographically, making it intrinsically more unfair than it is to begin with. A part of everyone's tax payments is being shipped to another state and given to another middle-class person who may have a *higher standard of living* than you. The trick is that he resides in an area where's it's cheaper to live. In its infinite ignorance, the federal government doesn't take cost of living into account.

Let's say you live in suburban New York, perhaps Nassau County on Long Island, have two children, and earn $35,000 a year. You're truly struggling because your small ranch house costs $225,000 and you're paying $5,000 a year in property taxes alone. You'll receive *no* EITC, thank you.

But—eat your heart out—the man in Little Rock, Arkansas, who earns only $20,000 a year is living as well as you, and is cashing in on free EITC green. His house costs only $100,000 and his local property taxes are only $1,000 a year. The cost of living in his area is 40 percent lower than yours. But to Uncle Sam, a tax is a tax is a tax, as is a tax credit.

The numbers come off a national, not local, tax table. The result is that while you'll receive no EITC, your Little Rock counterpart will get an annual check or tax credit of almost $2,000—part of which is coming out of your pocket!

That's only half the EITC problem. The other is fraud based on false income tax reports. It has reached epidemic proportions in EITC, as high as $6 billion a year.

In 1993 the new secretary of the treasury Lloyd Bentsen and IRS chief Margaret Richardson testified before Congress that an estimated 30–45 percent of EITC claims were a result of either error or cheating, what is called "noncompliance." In subsequent years the General Accounting Office followed up with two reports confirming the orgy of fraud in EITC.

The IRS did its own study, taking a sample of the 19,016,000 income tax returns, both electronic and paper, that claimed EITC benefits. They found that the paper returns *over-claimed* $2.795 billion, or 26 percent of the money, while the electronic returns wanted $1.645 billion more than they were entitled to, for a total of $4.44 billion. Today that same fraud rate would be almost $6 billion. Meanwhile, underclaims were a paltry 1.7 percent, indicating that fraud, not arithmetic, was usually the culprit.

Many taxpayers simply do not report under-the-table cash earnings. They declare only their official W-2 earnings, making them eligible for EITC money.

Multiple ingenious schemes have successfully outwitted the government. They include:

- A married couple files as if they are divorced, and both get the EITC check.

- Two single mothers who don't work pretend they are paying each other to take care of their children. They then file tax returns with almost nothing due the government but with EITC for both.

- People who have no children simply invent one or two kids, making them eligible for larger bonuses. (The maximum bonus for childless people is only $341, but it's $3,756 for a single parent with two children.)

- People get employer ID numbers, then file phony W-2 forms and collect the EITC cash bonuses for invented low-pay workers.

- Scammers copy other people's Social Security numbers, including those of children, and make fictitious EITC claims.

So rampant and obvious was the fraud that the IRS held up EITC checks for a while, trying to separate out the false claims. But since there are *millions of perpetrators* and the benefits have become sizable, only redesigning the entire program will cut the fraud. This is especially true since the typical EITC scam is for $2,000 while it costs $3,000 for an investigator to check out a case.

What happens if they catch you cheating? Will you go to jail? Heavens to Betsy, no. *In fact, after a suspension, you can even get back on the EITC rolls!*

Says the IRS in its eligibility booklet:

"Beginning in 1997, the earned income credit will be denied for a period of years if you improperly claim it because of reckless or intentional disregard of IRS rules or regulations, or *fraud* [italics mine]."

Fraud has become even more prevalent with electronic tax filing. The IRS set up a "Direct Deposit Indicator (DDI)" for these filers and within hours would notify them of the amount of the EITC free money. Soon banks and tax preparers were offering "anticipation loans," with the DDI information as collateral. Street gangs in Los Angeles even began preparing neighborhood tax returns for a cut of the EITC money.

The DDI system has been cut out and the IRS is attempting to increase surveillance of the massive fraud. In 1998 it asked for and received from Congress an additional $143 million to root it out, a small price *if* they can control the $6 billion a year that now goes down the EITC Beltway drain. But so far the great majority of the fraud goes on unabated, perhaps even increased.

What's the solution to this enormous waste?

1. Improve the IRS's low-tech computer system so that sophisticated software programs can snare many thieves *before* the EITC checks go out.

2. Reduce the maximum earnings permitted from $30,095 to $17,000 for a family of four—about the poverty level—eliminating millions from the program. There's no sense giving money out to people who make more than the average American. That will save billions and guarantee that only the needy working poor are being helped.

3. No EITC money or credit should go to people who have reasonable wealth: i.e. stock or liquid assets of more than $5,000.

4. The amount of investment income permitted each year should be zero.

5. Change the benefit equation to balance the difference in cost of living throughout the country. Connecticut is number one and Mississippi is number fifty, yet both get the same amount of EITC benefits per person. That makes no sense.

6. Eliminate the electronic filing for all EITC claimants. It has been proven to be an easier route to fraud.

7. Increase the criminal prosecutions for cheats as an example to the millions who now look upon EITC as a scammer's paradise—which, unfortunately, it is.

Implementing all seven of these recommendations would save taxpayers about half the $28 billion cost, or $14 billion, a nice piece of change.

Like so many government attempts to "help," EITC has backfired. In its askew regulations, waste, massive cost, and fraud, it has added still another burden on the working middle class, who—unlike EITC recipients—have to support a too often inefficient, falsely generous, impractical government.

It has to be controlled, but until then, I've got a beauty of a house in Little Rock I can sell you for $94,000. It comes with three bedrooms, two baths, and a built-in $2,000-a-year EITC annuity from those strange people up in Washington.

F

9

Federal Follies

More Aggravating Than Entertaining

In January 1999 the General Accounting Office issued a series of twenty small books, enumerating the errors of high-risk cabinet departments and agencies of the government. Reading the entire series is educational for the citizen, but perhaps I can choose a few highlights so that you can see how little Washington thinks of your tax money and how extravagant is their appetite for waste and foolishness.

HEALTH CARE FINANCING ADMINISTRATION (HCFA). State inspectors found that one in three nursing homes was providing inferior, often life-threatening, care. But HCFA's policies did not ensure that the poor care would be corrected.

FOOD SAFETY. One billion dollars a year was being spent to guard the quality of our food, but the work is inefficient and failing. Though food-borne disease claims as many as 9,100 deaths a year, the food safety operation suffers from inconsistent oversight and poor coordination. Duplication is rampant.

As many as twelve different federal agencies administer over thirty-five different laws overseeing food safety.

COMBATING TERRORISM. These programs suffer from the same ailment of wasteful and inefficient duplication. At a cost of $7 billion a year for just the unclassified programs to stop terrorism, over forty agencies, bureaus, and offices are in the act, making for very poor coordination.

NUCLEAR REGULATORY COMMISSION. This agency is responsible for our nuclear safety, but investigation revealed that the staff showed high levels of uncertainty and confusion about new regulations.

DEPARTMENT OF HOUSING AND URBAN DEVELOPMENT (HUD). Internal control weaknesses are costing us millions, even billions. The HUD budget included $517 million in items even though the contracts had expired, been terminated, or never been executed.

DEPARTMENT OF ENERGY. The agency has trouble completing large projects on time and within its budget. From 1980 through 1996, the DOE closed down thirty-one major projects costing over $100 million each after spending more than $10 billion. They completed only fifteen projects, most of them behind schedule and overbudget. For fifteen years they have worked on a permanent disposal site for radioactive waste at Yucca Mountain, Nevada. They have already spent $6.5 billion and the project is now twelve years behind schedule. The agency is not even sure the site is a suitable one for radioactive waste.

NATIONAL WEATHER SERVICE, DEPARTMENT OF COMMERCE. The $4.5 billion modernization program to better forecast weather is in grave trouble. The new radars were not always up and running when severe weather threatened. The ground-based sensors fell short on performance, especially when the weather was active. A NEXRAD (Next Generation Weather Radar) in Southern California was not always ready for use. The final piece of the modernization, AWIPS, or Advanced Weather Interactive Processing System, is far behind schedule and way overbudget. Originally planned to cost $350 million, it is now estimated at $618 million and is not fully ready after more than a dozen years.

DEPARTMENT OF AGRICULTURE. This massive organization has trouble downsizing. It still has twenty-seven hundred county offices that serve a declining number of full-time farmers, now estimated at only one million. This personalized service is now ridiculous considering that most farmers are "aggie" graduates and know more about farming than the county agents, many of whom major in rural sociology. Increasingly, farmers are dealing directly with centers in land grant colleges, which do most of the research in coordination with the states and federal government.

The Department has cut the number of county offices down by one thousand from its peak. It needs to cut out at least two thousand more. Of the 12,000 "field offices," only 2,000 have been closed. One office in Georgia handles a total of fifteen farmers, which prompted this macabre joke told in federal circles:

A Department of Agriculture bureaucrat came to work looking very depressed.

"What's wrong?" a fellow federal employee asked.

"I feel horrible. My farmer died."

FOOD STAMPS. Some $20 billion is spent each year providing food stamps for twenty-three million recipients. Fraud and abuse are rampant in the program because of overpayments to individuals and because of illegal trafficking in stamps for money or nonfood goods. In a recent year the government estimates that they overpaid $1.4 billion, which is surely an under-estimation. Thousands of prisoners, who are ineligible, received food stamps, as did deceased individuals.

FARM LOANS. The unpaid principal on only the *direct* loan portfolio is $9.7 billion, of which 28 percent, or $2.7 billion, is delinquent. One trying aspect of this program is that the government regularly forgives delinquent loans and writes off the losses. Then the government gives new loans to farmers who have failed to pay off prior ones. Ironically, or tragically, the government is finally limiting the number of times delinquent borrowers can receive debt forgiveness.

DEPARTMENT OF EDUCATION. One of its largest costs is providing and tracking student loans, which in one recent year totaled $48 billion given to 8.5 million students. But unfortunately, the department lacks the information necessary to budget and accurately estimate the size of the government's liability. In one recent year the government paid out $3.3 billion to make good its guarantee on defaulted student loans. The loan program is highly subject to waste and fraud, especially since the Department of Education can't always identify where a student is enrolled, even after a grant or loan is awarded.

DEPARTMENT OF THE INTERIOR. Four different groups—the National Park Service, the Bureau of Land Management, the Fish and Wildlife Service, and the Forest Service in the Department of Agriculture—handle several uncoordinated and duplicated activities. The agencies have been slow to improve. In one case they estimate that they need to do $7 billion of maintenance work, but that figure, says the GAO, "does not mean much, since they do not have accurate or reliable information on the extent of the problem."

In one case the Park Service maintains unused housing for

employees in one hundred parks when the need is not clear. The deferred maintenance on just these units costs as much as $200 million.

IMMIGRATION AND NATURALIZATION SERVICE. The INS has failed to check the criminal history of applicants for citizenship. As a result, it has falsely approved thousands with criminal backgrounds who should have been denied. Because INS seems incapable of performing the dual functions of protecting our borders and handling immigration and citizenship functions, it might be wise to dismantle the INS and replace it with another agency to handle immigration enforcement, while transferring immigration service to State and Labor.

AGENCY FOR INTERNATIONAL DEVELOPMENT. AID spends $6 billion a year and has projects in one hundred countries. However, the agency faces major performance challenges that threaten its ability to carry out its missions effectively. Its failure in management and information threatens such projects as the stock market trading system in Russia and the communications network in Egypt.

ENVIRONMENTAL PROTECTION AGENCY. The $7 billion budget is only the tip of the cost of complying with their regulations, which is estimated at $120 billion, or 1.5 percent of the entire gross domestic product. The agency's data systems are often outmoded. Its separately designed databases are not compatible with one another. Without this information, it is difficult for the EPA to set priorities. The agency, for example, has data on only one third of hazardous air pollutants. In addition, the EPA has had an uneven record in evaluating the success or failure of many of its projects.

The agency also has problems controlling the costs of contractors used to conduct cleanup in their Superfund program, making the program high-risk and vulnerable to waste, fraud, and abuse. One result is that the EPA has undercharged responsible parties in cleanups some $3 billion.

NATIONAL AERONAUTICS AND SPACE ADMINISTRATION. This agency, which spends $12 billion a year, seems to have a problem with costs and schedules. The cost of the International Space Station Program has increased $2 billion in three years to some $96 billion, and the final assembly date has slipped from June 2002 to December 2003.

DEPARTMENT OF LABOR. Data provided by the agency on the success of the $1 billion Job Corps program, which costs some $25,000 per participant, have been overblown and misleading. It is therefore difficult to have confidence in Labor's claims. While Labor reported that 48 percent of participants had completed a certain vocational training program, only 14 percent had actually completed the requirements. Labor's figures on the number who had obtained jobs after their training are also in question.

DEPARTMENT OF TRANSPORTATION, FEDERAL AVIATION ADMINISTRATION (FAA). The agency needs to improve its oversight of the aviation industry, especially in relation to airline and airport safety, and air traffic control. Its eighteen-year-long modernization of the air traffic control system, which will cost $42 billion through fiscal 2004, has experienced cost overruns, delays, and performance shortfalls of large proportions. The program is at high risk. The FAA process for acquiring software, the heart of the system, is ad hoc, sometimes chaotic, and not repeatable across projects. The FAA may not be able to deliver promised software on time and within budget.

FAA's organizational culture has impaired the acquisition process, and employees have acted in ways that did not reflect a strong enough commitment to mission focus.

There is substantial weakness in FAA's safety inspection of planes and repair facilities, which has been a factor in several accidents. There has not been sufficient documentation on whether the FAA has followed up on deficiencies inspectors had found. Many inspectors are not thorough or structured enough to detect many dangerous violations.

DEPARTMENT OF THE TREASURY, INTERNAL REVENUE SERVICE (IRS). The agency does not have sufficient security controls to prevent the loss of taxpayer money from theft, nor from inappropriate disclosure of taxpayer information. Receipts were left in unrestricted areas at IRS headquarters. Employees were hired and worked in areas where cash and checks were handled before the results of background and fingerprint checks were received.

Of eighty thefts the IRS investigated at service centers, twelve were committed by individuals who had previous arrests before their employment. Single unarmed couriers in ordinary civilian vehicles were used to transport millions of dollars during the peak filing season. One courier left a deposit totaling more than $200 million unattended in an open vehicle while he returned to the service center. At one district office, IRS relied on a bicycle messenger to deliver daily deposits ranging up to more than $100 million during the peak season.

And this is just a sampling of the federal follies starring your money. Read on.

10

Federal Palaces

$13 Million Just for the Architect?

When the government begins to build extravagant palaces with the people's money, as Saddam Hussein has, we know that democratic principles are in jeopardy. "Let them eat marble" should not become an American aphorism.

In Boston, where Supreme Court Justice Stephen Breyer once sat in a modest federal courthouse, there is now a glittering $218 million palace designed by I. M. Pei. "We looked for the best architect in the world," Breyer boasted. He did not come cheap. Pei's original bid was $8 million, but as the project unrolled, he raised his price to $13 million, all taxpayer-paid. Pei even spent $80,000 federal cash on a wooden model of the building.

The completed courthouse is the judiciary's Taj Mahal, more resplendent than the simple Greco-Roman home of the Supreme Court itself—yet surprisingly ugly. Centered around a lavish six-story atrium, and graced with the finest marbles, granites, and paneled woods, the building features thirty-three private kitchens, thirty-seven libraries, sixty-three private bathrooms, almost $1 million in art, and even a private dock on Boston Harbor.

But the cost of the building was less than half the actual tab. The site is way out of the way, virtually inaccessible to mainstream Boston. "It [the site] was rejected for transportation and litigation reasons," said a report by the Boston Redevelopment Authority.

But that was only a small problem for the fat federal purse, one that's much fuller than those of its citizens. Washington merely appropriated an additional $278 million for an extension of the Boston transit system so it could reach the courthouse! That sounds like a large tab, but at last count the cost of the underground railway has reached $601 million.

The "Palace Syndrome," also known as the "Edifice Complex," has the Washington politicians in its compulsive grip. You may be familiar with the Federal Triangle Project, the monster $800 million federal office building at Thirteenth and Pennsylvania Avenue. Though it was originally planned for $362 million, the price has doubled. No wonder the square footage costs for this building—which is second only to the Pentagon in size—rival those in midtown Manhattan.

Now called the Ronald Reagan International Trade Building, a name choice probably intended to sanitize the waste, it has little to do with trade. It has become mainly just another office building for the government bureaucracy. While federal employees are being moved into the unneeded palace, the General Services Administration admits that the government has 17,247,213 square feet of vacant office space elsewhere.

But if these two are monumental porkeries, they are bested by a planned new building for the Patent and Trademark Office (PTO). Scheduled to cost $13 billion, it will make the Reagan building look like a temporary shack.

That home of ingenuity will be most ingenious itself, replete with plazas, sculptures, decorative water fountains, walking and jogging trails, open-air amphitheaters, and programmable lighting control systems in every office space. Just the cost of moving into it is estimated at $120 million.

With all the talk of the era of big government being over, where are they getting the money to build the PTO palace? How could it get through Congress after the Triangle fiasco? Easy. In a clever piece of obfuscation, the Patent and Trademark Office is letting private industry build it. They're just *long-leasing* it for $50 million-plus a year (estimated cost, which will escalate greatly), giving the government zero equity over the long run. Money down the patent drain.

The epidemic of government building came to an abrupt halt in fiscal 1998 when both parties were posturing and bragging about "balancing the budget," which, as we've seen, has been a *virtual* event (see Chapter 3, Budget). That year no money was appropriated for new buildings, a propaganda ploy that was short-lived.

Then in fiscal 1999, over a half billion dollars was approved for some twenty new palaces, especially courthouses, part of a multibillion-dollar construction initiative that plans to build hundreds of new courtrooms to replace perfectly good ones now in use.

Once a city gets a new courthouse, other members of Congress lobby for one of their own. It's a contagious—and expensive—legislative disease, one in which jurists happily conspire.

In 1999 money was appropriated for the following courthouses:

- **Little Rock, AR, $3,436,000**

- **San Diego, CA, $15,400,000**

- San Jose, CA, $10,800,000
- Springfield, MA, $5,563,000
- Cape Girardeau, MO, $2,196,000
- Biloxi, MS, $7,543,000
- Eugene, OR, $7,190,000
- Greenville, TN, $26,517,000
- Laredo, TX, $28,105,000
- Wheeling, WV, $29,303,000

The last is the state of Senator Robert C. Byrd, the King of Pork, who, as former chairman of the Appropriations Committee, brought billions of his home state, including a $61 million courthouse in Charleston whose illuminated dome is 25 percent larger than the U.S. Capitol's!

The 1999 appropriation also included some mammoth courthouses:

- A lavish one in Jacksonville, FL, for $86,010,000. (Why the extra $10,000?)
- One in Brooklyn for $152,626,000!
- A federal building and courthouse expansion in Denver for $78 million.

Before the fake "moratorium" in 1998, the courthouse porkery was near continuous. In just two years, 1996 and 1997, Congress appropriated money for an additional twenty-five courthouses, including an "annex" in Tallahassee for $24 million; a federal building and courthouse in Lafayette, LA, for $30 million; the same in Omaha for $53 million; another in Scranton for $24 million; the same in Brownsville, TX, for $27 million; and the mother of them all, a federal building and courthouse in Central Islip, Long Island, for $189,102,000!

So ingrained is the courthouse conspiracy that when one public-spirited politician tried to stop it, he got hammered in the local press, which should know better. When a few years ago, Senator John McCain (R., AZ), the Senate's leading enemy of pork, complained that Phoenix didn't need the new $30 million courthouse—and that it was appropriated stealthily without ever having been "authorized"—he was lambasted by the state's largest daily newspaper. He even called on this author to write a letter to the editor opposing the building, something that proved futile in the mad spending atmosphere of Washington.

All this courthouse construction must mean that there is a shortage of federal courtrooms—that trials are being held around the clock in the federal judiciary, even in the halls. Right?

Absolutely wrong. A study by the General Accounting Office of courtroom usage in Denver, Fresno, Salt Lake, and Seattle, all sites getting new courthouses or expansions, turned up the dirty secret:

- On average, trials were being held in their courtrooms only 27 percent of the time.

- Nontrial use, for a short period of two hours or less, only 22 percent of the time.

- Nontrial use, for more than two hours, only 8 percent of the time.

Most important, the courtrooms were not being used at all 42 percent of the time. Trials were going on in them only a little more than a quarter of the time. Furthermore, all of the courtrooms at any of the four locations were often not used on the same day.

There is no need for additional courthouses, except in the political world of corrupt pork, one in which justices are now hand-in-robe with politicians.

What to do?

All appropriations for new courthouses should be rescinded, and no new ones made.

A five-year moratorium should be put into effect on all new federal buildings, including the proposed new extravagance, the Patent and Trademark monster. The vacant space in federal buildings, which represents as much office space as in a medium-sized city, should be used up before another nickel is spent.

The savings will be in the multibillions. Perhaps most important, it might scale back the errant thinking of wasteprone politicians.

Maybe. *But don't bet your city's own courthouse on it.*

G

11

Golf

Putts Instead of Planes

Everyone knows (or should know) that our armed forces have taken a budget beating since our stunning victory in the Gulf War. Since 1991, when our active military numbered over two million, the ranks have been cut so badly that we are being defended—rather lightly—by only 1.4 million service people.

Take the Air Force. Its roster has dropped from over 600,000 in 1986 to some 360,000 today, with a similar hit on its flying power. "Our fighter and bomber strength has been reduced almost 40 percent since Desert Storm," a Pentagon spokesman lamented.

But take heart, brave Americans. As the power of our defense structure continues to be depleted—perhaps dangerously—one wing of the armed forces continues to show real strength.

Where is that? On the sea, in the air? No, silly patriot. The drive for dominance is where Congress and the Pentagon apparently believe it's most important—on the military golf links.

Not only are there 196 golf courses in the military command, but their strength is growing. Recently Andrews Air Force Base built its *third* golf course at a cost of over $5 million. "The Andrews courses are very crowded," explained an Air Force spokesman. "We needed more facilities to handle the demand."

Why? If there are fewer Air Force personnel, where is the demand? And why still more golf courses?

The answer is that Andrews is conveniently located just eleven miles from the ground zero of federal perkdom—Washington, D.C. On any given weekend, you are likely to find a congressman rather than an underpaid Air Force sergeant teeing off on the taxpayers' dollar.

How come? Because Andrews's golf courses are open not only to top gunners but to members of Congress and staff, and all civilian workers of the Pentagon. To call it a "military" golf course disguises its real purpose—to provide still another taxpayer-paid perk for Washington VIPs.

"Andrews is becoming the golf mecca of Washington, D.C.," says Rep. Peter DeFazio (D., OR), who tried unsuccessfully to block the construction of the new links. "I don't think you need a third eighteen-hole golf course for Washington's elite."

Representatives Christopher Shays (R., CT), David Minge (D., MN), and Jack Metcalf (R., WA) joined DeFazio in a protest to the Secretary of Defense, but it proved futile.

The cost of golf for VIPs is humorously cheap. For a paltry $30 greens fee, America's politicians and their civilian staffs can play their eighteen holes. Much cheaper, we should add, than the multithousand-dollar initiation and yearly membership fee, and the $75 daily greens fee, at Burning Tree, one of the private clubs that other big shots must support out of their own pockets.

Until recently, members of Congress had open access to

military golf clubs, but after criticism (including exposure by this author), they now have to ask permission from an Air Force liaison officer. Not surprisingly, no one has been turned down.

The Pentagon claims that the military courses are self-supporting, which is nonsense, what DeFazio calls "an accounting trick." The Defense Department morale and recreation program, which supports it, is in bad shape financially. The fund receives nearly a billion dollars a year in tax subsidies, part of which goes for the upkeep of the courses.

"There is no question that we subsidize these courses," said former Senator Dennis DeConcini of Arizona. "They are on public lands and pay no taxes."

The solution?

It makes no sense to give golf perks to VIP civilians, including members of Congress and their staffs, on military golf courses. Eliminate that privilege—by law. Let them do what everyone else does, pay for play, elsewhere.

Also, we might follow up on a plan that was knocked down a few years ago. One congressman suggested that those links that were underused outside the Beltway might cater to the paying public, bringing in an estimated $100 million a year.

If we don't do that, we should turn the courses *exclusively* back to the soldiers, sailors, and airmen.

Since their ranks are being decimated, we should be able to close, not expand, unneeded golf courses.

We'll be saving millions on every swing.

H

12

Horses

Millions for Belgian Steaks

"Adopt a living legend," the recording says once you've called a federal agency at 1-800-417-9647, toll-free.

The adoption is not for a baby to fill a childless home. Instead it is a call for Americans to adopt a beautiful, mighty wild horse from the western hills and plains for the bargain price of $125.

Sound good? Of course, except that we forget that somewhere in virtually every federal scheme is a mountain of waste—or stupidity. The horse plan, which has cost the government a quarter of a *billion* dollars since it began in 1971, is no exception.

Between the romantic image of wild horses happily roaming free in herds and the reality is a sordid tale of Washington's mismanagement, even unintentional inhumanity.

Ever since Congress passed the "Wild Free Roaming Horse and Burro Act," the Bureau of Land Management (BLM) of the Department of the Interior—the largest landlord in America—has paid to corral 165,000 horses and prepare them for adoption. The rationale is reasonable. The horses multiply mightily, and in the winter there isn't enough forage grass to feed the herds. The horses had to be saved from a miserable fate of starvation.

Helicopters, playing modern cowboys, swoop down on the horses and direct them to pens as they run away from the whirlies. Once captured, they are branded and vaccinated at a cost to taxpayers of some $1,100 per horse. The adoption process then begins, generally with a BLM auction, held regularly around the country with a general price of $150. The new owner takes final title after a year of "humane" ownership. In fact, each citizen can adopt as many as four horses over a period of a year.

So what happens to these once free "living legends"? Do they spend the rest of their natural lives in friendly pastures, nurtured by loving children and families?

No way. In fact, the worst of fates awaits most of them as the proud animals end up on somebody's dinner plate in Europe!

A follow-up by the Associated Press of several dozen "adopted" federal horses revealed that they had been butchered. They had been sold by their supposedly humane adopters to slaughterhouses only to end up as *Tournedos du chevaux*, the filet mignon of *horsemeat* in restaurants in France and Belgium, where the flesh is prized.

At a slaughterhouse in Oregon, the proprietor explained that the horses are "killed on Friday, processed on Monday. Thursday we load the truck and then it's flown to Europe."

What does the BLM say? Do only a few adopted federal horses end up as delicacies for the Continental palate? Hardly. The director of the wild-horse program admits that about 90 percent of them are sold for slaughter by their new owners. Their meat is prized in Europe because, unlike the usual slaughtered horses, which are old or infirm, the "adopted" horses off the plains are young and healthy.

"Talk about the waste of public funds," said former Senator Clifford Hansen of Wyoming, who introduced the original bill, and who lamented the $17-million-a-year cost.

Taxpayers may blanch at the waste, as they should. But how about the fate of those once wild and free horses whose lives had been foolishly entrusted to Uncle Sam?

The solution: save the remaining forty-three thousand wild horses and burros on the range—and much of the $17 million a year—by dropping forage to them by the same helicopter used to capture them.

Or change the law. Require the owners who adopt the horses to maintain them for at least five years, or pay a fine triple what they could get for the horsemeat.

And incidentally, the next time you visit Paris or Brussels, please watch what you eat. You may have already paid for that steak with your tax money.

I

13

International Enterprise Funds

Want to Buy a Mutual Fund—in Bulgaria?

Has your mutual fund made a few dollars for you over the last years?

Probably.

The idea of an investment fund taking an equity position in companies is an old proven idea that in the *private sector* has worked like gangbusters.

So why not, Uncle Sam said, help out businesses in the new democracies of Eastern Europe by setting up investment funds that would invest in local businesses or start new ones?

It's not only good foreign policy, but it would make a few dollars for the U.S. government, they said. Wasn't everybody making money in the go-go financial world?

Who would back this unusual concept of Washington going into a venture capital operation—one that would actually compete with private investment banks? Naturally, the American taxpayer. But, said Washington, they won't mind because one of the goals was to make money for Uncle Sam.

Considering booming stock markets, that shouldn't be too difficult, the bureaucrats said.

With taxpayer money, "enterprise funds" were set up, mainly in Eastern Europe, by two government agencies: the Agency for International Development (AID) and the Overseas Private Investment Corporation. The kitty was $1.32 billion, and the funds included:

- Czech and Slovak American Enterprise Fund
- Polish-American Enterprise Fund
- U.S.-Russia Investment Fund
- Hungarian-American Enterprise Fund
- Central Asian–American Enterprise Fund
- Bulgarian-American Enterprise Fund
- Romanian-American Enterprise Fund
- Baltic-American Enterprise Fund
- Albanian-American Enterprise Fund
- Western NIS (Newly Independent States) Enterprise Fund

Private mutual funds in emerging European countries have been doing nicely. So how about Uncle Sam's efforts?

Not so good. In fact, quite poorly, as one would expect. Of the $1.32 billion authorized, $952 million has already been committed as direct investment in businesses or as loans.

What are the international enterprise funds worth today? An official of the agency claims that there is no way to calculate the value, but a consultant on the enterprise funds was more candid. *He estimated that their investment is worth only about* *sixty cents on its original $1 of cost. They have already suffered a loss of $280 million, with more red ink to come!*

In fact, the first definitive results include what the AID spokesman calls "an absolute disaster." That involves the Czech and Slovak fund, especially the Czech portion. Begun in 1990, it had a seed investment of $65 million. Most of the money expended was put into loans to manufacturing firms, which has generally been a successful field in Czechoslovakia. But most were start-ups, which is itself a dangerous idea in the venture capital world.

What happened? *The fund was closed in 1997, recouping only eleven cents on the dollar, a loss of 89 percent of its investment!*

Harvey Schuster, who heads Corus Funds, a private mutual fund in Prague, says the Washington failure was a case of "the blind leading the blind. The Czechs didn't know how to manage and the Americans didn't know how to invest."

Two former board members say the board "was essentially unwilling to aggressively administer the bitter medicine of capitalism where it was warranted."

Some of the problem was Washington's flawed design of the project to begin with. By law, the majority of the board of directors of these foreign operations must be American. They are also political appointees—who suffer the liability of that whole class. Furthermore, and this makes absolutely no sense, the CEOs of the local operations are not locals, but Americans.

"Most of the CEOs of our funds—who earn up to $150,000 a year—do not speak the language, nor do they usually live in the countries involved," says the AID spokesman. "A number of them are Wall Street types and they prefer to live in the United States or in the capitals of Western Europe and just visit the area they're handling."

Doug Bandow of the CATO Institute, a prominent Washington think tank, points out that the Central Asian–American Enterprise Fund boasts that their board is composed of "distinguished members of the American business and academic communities." What, he asks, "do distinguished academics know about investing in the Kirgiz Republic?"

The Russian fund, like several others, has suffered enormous losses in its $440 million portfolio, with only one notable success, the Star Brewery. An AID spokesman estimates that the fund is now worth less than $100 million, *having lost over three fourths of the original investment.*

One reason for the general failure of the funds was summed up by the General Accounting Office, which said that "the level of understanding of business practices at the companies in which they invested was lower than they originally thought."

Another reason was top-heavy expenses, a failing of those who have had too much exposure to our government culture. "Perks before results," as one AID official said. An AID inspector general agreed, finding that expenses were excessively high. The Bulgarian Fund expenses ran 23 percent of its total outlay, while it was 26 percent in the Hungarian fund, both of which are losing money. He also added: "Fund officials complained of high legal fees . . . Some reported that they had received invoices for services that were never requested."

Even over there, Uncle Sucker is noted for his propensity to waste money.

Have there been any successes among the ten funds?

Yes, Poland. That nation's enterprise fund has actually been *making money.* Not a lot, but some. Our original investment of $256 million was recently worth some $265 million, said an AID consultant, a small gain that he believes portends good things for the fund, an exception in a cascade of red ink.

What then to do with the $1.4 billion authorized by Congress?

1. Save the remaining millions not yet spent and close down the whole operation.

2. Change the rules so that the CEO of each fund must not only be a proven professional in investing, but speak the local language.

3. The CEO should be required to live in the capital of the country in which our money is being invested.

4. The expense-to-revenue ratio should be cut in half.

5. Turn the whole thing over to the Poles.

Will any of that work if we keep the funds open?

Probably not. The U.S. government is famous for its chutz-pah, for its unparalleled optimism that programs will work when they do not have the intellectual capital or the discipline to make them succeed.

A frank AID staffer summed it up: "We'd be giving them money anyway—we might as well try to make a few dollars in the process."

Lotsaluck.

14

Junkets, Military Style

Fly Me to the Moon

When an Arkansas House member went on a junket to warm San Juan, Puerto Rico, with colleagues and staff, the Pentagon eagerly provided the plane along with military escorts to make life luxurious for the "codel," Defense Department lingo for "congressional delegation."

Luxury is what they got. The member and his entourage and some guests, a total of twenty-two people, sat down to dinner at the swank Caribe Hilton Hotel. The tab came to $1,638, of which the Pentagon—meaning the taxpayers—picked up nearly $1,000, the official portion of the feast. The next night, twenty-one people connected to the codel ate $1,321 worth, with $948 coming from the taxpayers.

This is Nirvana for a congressional junketeer. It is not on his budget and he doesn't have to account for it. It is shifted to the budget of the Pentagon, which is a massive swamp where a dozen CPAs could never isolate the cost. Why? Because this is public relations money, cash expended to influence the people—members of Congress—who write the military budget. A dollar spent courting their civilian bosses could return thousands in appropriations.

Is it done much? Only continually.

In still another "perky" trip by members and their staffs, a Virginia senator visited the Middle East for a week with a congressional aide and a military escort. They were flown there on military planes, and once ensconced in the region, their escort proved to be as generous with our nickel as Congress has proven to be. The Pentagon escort reportedly gave maids $50 tips and spent $179 for baggage tips for only three travelers.

This was penny-ante compared with a congressional entourage which went to China with a Pennsylvania House member. The taxpayer-paid tip total? Try $2,000!

Members of Congress travel free on military planes, and have their hotels and meals taken care of very nicely, luxury that they consider commensurate with their status. One Pennsylvania senator has earned the reputation of being a persnickety military traveler. When he flies on the public's money, he gives the Pentagon a detailed list for his meals, including Healthy Choice vanilla ice cream and Familia/Swiss muesli, original recipe. One time he wired ahead to have an air-conditioned squash court ready for him in a foreign capital.

Members of Congress and their spouses are usually picked up at the Capitol by a military van from Andrews Air Force Base and taken to their plane, which is always well stocked with liquor, whether people drink or not. The alcohol perk—wine, beer, or scotch—is important to the Pentagon, which is quite eager to please members of Congress with your money.

On a junket led by an Alaskan senator, with ten other congressional officials, military escorts brought $1,500 in liquor with them, including seventy-three bottles of wine. An earlier such trip to the Middle East involved a $1,400 alcohol buy even before the plane left the ground.

"This is money that's supposed to be spent on national security," says Tom Schatz, president of the six-hundred-thousand-member watchdog organization Citizens Against Government Waste. "I'm not sure what indulging in alcohol will do to preserve the country."

In a three-part detailed report, *The Hill*, a publication that covers Congress, recently explored the travels of junket-mad members who use military planes to accomplish their freebie goals. In fact, there is no limit on the amount of money traveling members can spend.

An Alabama House member capped off an official business trip in Europe by boarding a military plane with several colleagues for a three-day all-expense-paid vacation to Athens. He was there with five other members of the House and their spouses, from both parties. They made the tour of the Acropolis and stayed at the Astir Palace, Greece's premier hotel, HQ for their supposed investigation of "human rights."

Prior to that, they stayed in Istanbul and cruised the Bosporus after visits to such famed sights as Topkapi Palace.

This "codel" cost the taxpayers $3,000 an hour for the use of a C-22 transport, plus at least another $5,000 for the three days in Athens.

On overseas trips, members generally bring along their spouses under the guise of fulfilling "protocol" needs. But one aide commented that they're mainly out shopping.

Members will apparently use any excuse to get their freebie junkets. Members of the House Agriculture Committee went to a tourist city in Mexico to investigate "livestock." The Senate Select Committee on Intelligence arranged a taxpayer-paid bus trip to Gettysburg to understand battlefield intelligence. The Pentagon liked the idea so much that they set up trips for congressional aides to the Antietam battlefield in Maryland—including breakfast and picnic lunch—at $1,538 per tour.

What can we do to stop this unaccounted-for freeloading? Simple.

1. The trips should be announced in the press, both national and in the members' home district or state, prior to takeoff, listing all the freebie passengers and where they're going and for how long.

2. The cost of the trip, including the $3,000 an hour for the military plane, should be outlined in that release.

3. No spouses should be allowed to travel free of charge since this is ostensibly a government "business trip."

4. The Pentagon should not be allowed to provide military "escorts" for the members' convenience.

5. The money spent should be charged—not to the Pentagon's fiscal swamp—but to the member's representational allowance so that it reduces what he can spend on other things, including mass mailings.

Under those conditions, let's see how many happy voyagers will elect to travel overseas on the Pentagon's—meaning mine and your—nickel.

K

15

Kickbacks, Bribes, Con Jobs, and Simple Fraud

Uncle Sucker Gets Ripped Off, Inside and Out

Three clerks in the CIA decided that the federal government was easy pickings. Because of their inside position at Langley, they were able to monitor the movement of overseas agents, especially the credit cards being sent around the world to make the spies' lives easier.

Their plan was simple: they just shortstopped 108 credit cards—Visa, Master, and Diners Club—and used them for their own enjoyment.

By the time they were caught, they had spent $160,000 of Uncle Sam's money on wild shopping sprees for satellite dishes, thirty-two-inch color television sets, car tires, a sixty-disc CD system, even tickets to the Washington Wizards basketball games. To make *their* lives easier, they took $30,000 in cash advances from the cards.

One would think that with all the bureaucratic red tape, bilking the federal government would be difficult. Quite the opposite is true, and the work of inspectors general in every agency confirms it. But we have to assume that for each fraud they uncover, ten thieves get away.

No one knows the exact toll of fraud on the government, but an estimate of $50 billion a year is probably quite conservative.

The fraud comes from both federal employees on the inside and contractors and the public on the outside, all eager to get in line for their part of the $2 *trillion* annual federal buffet.

One agency that is a favorite target of both inside and outside crooks is the General Services Administration, a "housekeeping" giant that handles a great deal of procurement for other government agencies, federal buildings in general, surplus government property, and such odds and ends as cars and civilian government aircraft. The reason it's such a perfect target is not only its size but that it is considered one of the worst-managed agencies in Washington.

Its multiple frauds keep its efficient, if understaffed, inspector general working. Here are just some of the "inside" jobs by criminal GSA employees:

- One GSA building manager decided to have it both ways—keep his good salary and tap into the agency for his own outside private business, which was building private homes. He was suspended for conflict of interest when it was learned he used an electrical contractor on a GSA job to wire his houses.

- An Army recruiter used a GSA gasoline credit card to rip off $1,960 by conspiring with gas station attendants to inflate the gasoline buys, then split the difference in cash. He was sentenced to two years of probation. The IG learned about the racket when it was discovered that he was billing for more than the car's sixteen-gallon gas tank capacity.

- An employee in a GSA distribution warehouse pled guilty to stealing $240,000 in tools meant for several government agencies. The IG tracked him down when it was discovered that the tools were selling on the black market for less than the discounted manufacturer's price.

- One GSA employee directed GSA and VA contracts for $50,000 worth of paint to a supply company, for which he received a kickback of $2,100.

- A Tennessee state trooper, the director, and a captain of the troops obtained surplus property from GSA warehouses, claiming it was to be used for a rescue squad, which enabled them to get it free of charge. Instead, they transported the property, worth $682,600, to a commercial surplus store owned by the trooper and sold it to the public. They were all caught and prosecuted.

- Eight GSA employees entered into a conspiracy to steal government property from a GSA distribution center. The scam was discovered when one of the crooks sold the property to another employee, who became suspicious because it was still in the original container with a GSA stock number. Of the eight GSA thieves, two were placed on probation and fined, and four resigned—ostensibly still keeping their pensions.

- A GSA employee supervising a contractor working on a government sewage facility tried to extort a $25,000 bribe from the contractor. The FBI and the IG investigated and found that the government employee had already accepted a $5,000 down payment. In return, the GSA employee was to provide the contractor with information that would enable him to submit fraudulent payment claims to the GSA. The contractor cooperated with the FBI and set up a meeting in which the employee accepted another $5,000, after which he was arrested. He was sentenced to fifteen months in prison.

- GSA briberies do not just involve ordinary federal employees, but officials as well. In one large scam, a motor transportation officer—who supervised operations of a regional government fleet of cars—worked with an automotive repair inspector in a three-part scheme: (1) the vendor, a car-repair company, submitted inflated claims to the GSA officer, who approved them, then took cash for the difference between the inflated claim and true cost; (2) they solicited cash that was supposed to be for two holiday parties for GSA employees, but instead kept the money; (3) they took cash sporadically along with free service for their own cars. The GSA transportation officer took $1,350 along with free service. The inspector also gave the vendors confidential bidding information for which he got $18,850 and free service. The transportation officer resigned and the inspector was fined. The forgiving government did not charge either man with a crime.

Not all agencies have as many blatantly crooked employees as the GSA, of which we've shown only a sample, but fraud among federal employees is still commonplace.

Another leading center of federal connivance is the Department of Justice, especially its drug and immigration enforcement.

- An Immigration and Naturalization Service (INS) supervisory cashier clerk arranged for a middleman to print counterfeit payroll checks, which were cashed using INS documents as ID. The clerk was given six months home confinement.

- An undercover investigator in the New York area learned that over a four-year period, five INS employees took bribes to issue green cards, or work permits, to illegal aliens, charging from $300 to $1,000 per card. When arrested, the middleman "vendor" was found with over $164,000 in cash.

- In New Jersey, an INS agent, a clerk, and three civilian documents sellers were arrested. For $4,000, the federal agent had sold them the template used to prevent forgeries of Resident Alien and Border Crossing cards.

- A deputy U.S. marshal collected over $300,000 in salary and benefits—while he was operating a private travel business in Peru. He was sent to jail for one year for his fraud.

- The San Diego field offices of the FBI and U.S. Customs, working on a drug investigation, found that corrupt INS and Customs inspectors were helping drug dealers bring cocaine into the United States. The government recovered $1,222,345 in drug profits.

- In the District of Columbia, a government recreation specialist was arrested for bringing narcotics into a prison facility. He was paid to smuggle marijuana into the jail in detergent boxes.

- Also in D.C., a Justice Department mail clerk set up a system in which he stole boxes of bank checks and gave them to civilian coconspirators in exchange for television and video equipment.

- In South Carolina, an INS adjudication officer was arrested for helping aliens become citizens illegally. He accepted bribes from document brokers to certify that Chinese and Vietnamese aliens had passed the English language test when in fact they couldn't read or write English.

- In the Eastern District of New York, a nineteen-month investigation, code-named Operation Badfellas, resulted in the arrest of eleven Bureau of Prisons correctional officers. They accepted bribes to make life easy for prisoners by smuggling in contraband, including drugs and food. They also took bribes so that organized-crime inmates could live together and continue their mob planning from jail.

No federal agency is exempt from "inside" fraud. The Social Security Administration has its own internal thieves.

- One employee in Florida was sentenced to thirty-three months in jail for issuing Social Security numbers illegally.

- In another Florida case, the FBI and the Border Patrol found that a coconspirator paid a federal employee $80,000 over a period of time for obtaining valid Social Security cards for illegal aliens.

- A federal hearing clerk in the Eastern District of Louisiana was convicted of taking bribes to give favorable opinions in Social Security cases.

- One Social Security employee came up with an ingenious scheme. She created a fictitious human being and gave "her" a real Social Security number. With that she received credit cards. Her scheme tumbled when she was stopped by a policeman for traffic reasons and showed her fake SSN (Social Security number).

The outside scams are just as common as insider fraud. Crooks tap numerous farm programs, including the crop insurance or "Risk Management" division of the Department of Agriculture, which takes in $1.8 billion a year in premiums. Seventeen Louisiana farmers found that pool of cash attractive and defrauded the government of $1.5 million by claiming nonexistent losses.

(Sometimes there's no fraud, just sloppy bookkeeping. On audit it was learned that the famous King Ranch collected nearly $1 million extra in crop insurance payments—15 percent over their $7.3 million payout.)

Contractors working for the government find Washington an easy target. We know that because at least one *honest* contractor has told officials to tighten its sloppy procedures if they want to stop the flow of fraud.

For thirty years a Chevy Chase, Maryland, carpet firm kept refunding money to the government—overpayments they received for work done. In many cases they were paid twice by several agencies, including the IRS. The company's president wrote the government several times saying that many other firms were keeping the government overpayments—committing fraud.

He was obviously on to something.

At the General Services Administration, the IG is kept quite busy. Just a few of the outside scams by contractors who are insufficiently supervised by the GSA include:

- A typewriter and photography supplier had to pay $1.8 million back to the GSA after it violated its pricing contract. The first estimate was that it had overcharged the agency $505,490 over a four-year period, but the IG's investigation showed the fraud was much larger.

- A computer manufacturer ripped off the GSA (so what's new?) by selling them reconditioned computers instead of new ones as contracted. They had to pay back $14.8 million, the amount they got away with—plus more.

- A distributor of scientific laboratory equipment agreed to pay the government $1.5 million after an IG audit showed that the firm did not disclose the *common* fact that they were selling to private customers at larger discounts than they were giving the GSA, a violation of their contract.

The contractor scam is so universal that it would require an army of IG investigators to even pierce its surface. The Department of Defense is a prime victim (or a prime sucker), as these recent cases involving major defense contractors illustrate:

- Pratt & Whitney, the engine manufacturer, agreed to pay $14.8 million after it was learned that, says the IG of Defense, they "violated the False Claims Act by preparing false purchase orders and submitted false invoices under the Foreign Military Sales Program."

- The Boeing Company made a $6 million settlement in connection with work on the Boeing 777 program, by shifting some of their civilian costs into their government account. Says the IG: "Costs related to this commercial program were included in Governmental General and Administrative accounts." Boeing had used these false numbers to determine their overhead for government work.

- CTK International, Incorporated, was given a $2 million fine for supplying Defense with monitors that were mislabeled to make it look as if they were manufactured—as part of the Buy American Act—in "compliant" countries when they were really made elsewhere.

- Organized-crime elements were involved in the purchase and sale of over $8 million in fuel stolen from a defense fuel supply center. The leader was sentenced to forty-one months in jail.

When it comes to outsider fraud, perhaps the largest criminal element is ordinary citizens who see the loose largesse of Washington as the perfect target.

As we have seen, the Earned Income Tax Credit is an open sewer of citizen fraud, running just ahead of Social Security ripoffs—such as the following:

- A billing clerk at a medical center in Texas used false SSNs to set up bank accounts to deposit fraudulent Medicare payments she arranged to get. In all, $159,700 was involved.

- Three individuals in Alabama used fake names and fake SSNs to get student loans of such magnitude that they had to make restitution of $95,319.

- Collecting Social Security checks after the recipient has passed away is a favorite fraud. One man in Louisiana pled guilty to eighteen counts of fraud after the IG received a tip that his mother was deceased. The thief hid her death for five years, collecting and cashing $35,862 in illegal Social Security checks.

- In New York, a sixty-five-year-old woman was sentenced to three years of probation and had to make $92,559.80 in restitution for cashing her mother's Social Security checks for *fourteen years after her death!* They discovered the fraud because on the dead woman's supposed hundredth birthday, Social Security sought a face-to-face visit, which obviously never took place.

Two of the other massive scams operated by citizens include Medicare and food stamp frauds, which together approach $30 billion a year.

The Medicare and Medicaid fraud covers the entire spectrum of thievery, which includes hospital overcharges, nursing-home fake billing, and false claims by home health providers and medical equipment sellers, especially for the aged. One of the largest frauds involves our family doctors and specialists, thousands of whom regularly "upcode" their Medicare insurance forms. Physicians simply claim they did more for the patient than they actually did, bringing them anywhere from $10 to $100 more per visit, heavily padding their incomes.

The inspector general of the Department of Health and

Human Services estimates that there is $23 billion in medical fraud against the federal government, which is surely an understatement.

Another giant, perpetual, minute-to-minute scam carried on by millions of Americans is food stamp fraud, or as one critic calls it, "out of the mouths of babes."

What started out as a small program in 1964 as part of the Great Society has mushroomed to a $28 billion one with some thirty million beneficiaries. As the program has grown, so has the volume of fraud, which is now estimated at over $5 billion a year.

Scamming the food-stamp program is virtually effortless since the stamps act as a form of "underground currency." They sell for anywhere from thirty to fifty cents on the dollar in the black market, and are either redeemed with the government for the full dollar, or are used by drug dealers and money launderers as if they were cash. Since the law prohibits the use of food stamps to purchase alcohol or cigarettes, many housewives shortchange their families by exchanging the stamps for cash instead of feeding their children.

Some of the more exotic anecdotes of fraud include:

- Using food stamps to buy handguns.
- Undercover agents in Wisconsin used the stamps as a down payment on a house.
- In 1993, during the Missouri flood, the USDA issued $5.5 million in emergency food stamps to victims. The misuse of much of it was documented when twelve operators of retail grocery stores dealing in the stamps pled guilty to fraud. Some of the thieves got away with it because an informant was murdered.

- One food-stamp recipient traveled from state to state by bus, eventually qualifying to receive stamps in seventeen states, defrauding the government of $18,000 before he was finally caught.

- Even though a grocery store in Saint Louis was closed for business, it continued to redeem food stamps illegally, buying them at a huge discount from eligible poor people.

- Many stores are really fronts for illegal food-stamp dealing. One store exposed by the IG had the following skimpy grocery inventory: a cooler containing an open carton of buttermilk, an open package of bologna, a couple of boxes of cereal, and a few other items. Yet it was redeeming $1,400 a month in food stamps.

How widespread is the racket?

An officer of the Michigan State Police says that he sees about one in four people who come out of his local food-stamp distribution center trade their stamps for cash and not for food. "They walk outside and quickly sell the little coupons at a discount to organized rings of cocky street hawkers and crooked grocers, who will redeem the stamps at full value for a neat profit from the U.S. government."

The thieves even exploit new mothers who receive extra food for their newborns under the WIC (Women, Infants, and Children) program. In Georgia, three crooks pled guilty to illegally redeeming $1.5 million in food stamps, including $328,000 in WIC coupons sold to them by mothers who took the cash instead of feeding their children.

Although it is not foolproof as thieves learn to deal with new electronic methods, some cities are involved in a test of electronic transfer in which the recipient has a food-stamp card instead of coupons. The machine deducts the eligibility each time it's used and will hopefully cut back the enormous fraud.

The extent of fraud in the federal government is almost as large a problem as waste, and the two are in certain ways intertwined. The general failure of rigor, of accounting, of accountability, and of the lack of determination to do the best possible job at the lowest cost infects Washington from top to bottom.

To cleanse the fraud situation requires a general new overview of the government, something we will attempt in Part Three.

Until then, the best advice is: Don't scam the government, and try to stop those who do.

L

16

Loans

The Government Bank: Everyone's Welcome

As we've seen in Chapter 3, Budget, the national debt continues to rise despite the so-called surplus being brazenly announced by Washington. By the year 2004 the debt will probably have reached $6 trillion, a frightening specter.

Does that mean that $6 trillion is the limit of the national indebtedness? Are there some odds and ends that we also owe that the government isn't talking about?

Yes, and more than odds and ends. *In fact, the national debt is only one third the real fiscal obligation of the federal government, which is now a frightening $18 trillion, or nine times the annual cost of government. The rest is cleverly hidden from the taxpayer by keeping it off-budget.*

Uncle Sam has flung himself into an orgy of direct lending, guaranteeing loans, dealing in unfunded obligations, and handing out insurance to private organizations, willy-nilly, rolling up liabilities quicker than at any time in our history.

To whom do we owe the money, and from what stream of

bureaucracy? Virtually everyone and from everywhere. And the system is far from foolproof.

Remember the S & L insurance bailout of depositors that cost us $200 billion? And a smaller $4 billion loss at the Federal Housing Administration, which insures mortgages? The Export-Import Bank has "sustained large losses over the past decade," the government has admitted. Students are not well known for their credit-worthiness, and each year about one in nine fails to pay back his or her loan to Uncle Sam.

This is just the tip of the possible losses. The list of programs that depend on Uncle Sam's credit and credit guarantees—which means me and you to the tune of $700,000 for each family of four—is virtually endless. The money is at risk in five areas: bank deposit insurance; loans and guarantees; pension programs; direct loan programs; government-sponsored enterprises.

The loan programs include:

- Over a trillion dollars in savings and loan deposits insured by the government.
- Almost three trillion dollars in deposits at commercial and savings banks insured by the FDIC.
- Almost a trillion in guaranteed VA and FHA mortgages.
- $21 billion just in direct student loans.
- $100 billion for Federal Family Education student loans.
- $34 billion in rural electrification and telephone loans.
- Agency for International Development, $13 billion.
- Maritime loans of several hundred million.
- $35 billion for the Small Business Administration.

- Farm Service Agency and Rural Development, $47 billion.

- Foreign Military Financing, $8 billion.

- Millions in flood insurance guarantees.

- $40 billion in Export-Import Bank loans and guarantees.

- Almost a trillion dollars in guarantees behind the Pension Benefit Guaranty Corporation, which insures workers' pensions.

- Millions for college housing loans.

- Billions in Overseas Private Investment Corporation insurance for American firms against political upheaval.

- Several supposedly private enterprises that are actually government-sponsored and implicitly insured for some $1.7 *trillion* dollars. These include the Federal National Mortgage Association (Fannie Mae); Farm Credit System; the Federal Home Loan Bank System; Federal Home Loan Mortgage Corporation; and the Student Loan Marketing Association (Sally Mae).

Washington has not been honest about this giant debt looming over our fiscal future. But they do give it a nod in the "Analytic Perspectives" section of the five-part federal budget

"The federal government continues to be the largest financial institution in the United States . . . The total federal and federally assisted credit and insurance outstanding is $7.9 trillion," the budget states.

That's fine as far as it goes, but the $7.9 trillion plus the 1998 national debt of $5.5 trillion equals $13.5 trillion, which is about $5 trillion short of the *real* amount, says the National Taxpayers Union. That organization does a regular accounting of the total debt, what they call the "Taxpayer's Liability Index" (TLI), now over $18 trillion and growing faster than any aspect of the Beltway mayhem.

In 1972 the TLI was only $2.04 billion and by 1975 had reached $5 billion, then $10 billion by 1981, then $15 billion by 1991, and $18 billion by 1996. It hasn't been measured since and is surely nipping at the $20 billion mark.

What should we do?

First, declare a moratorium on all future loans and guarantees, except for student loans, where collection from defaulters has to be tightened—using the IRS. Then we should start to collect more of the outstanding money, and most important, close down dozens of lending agencies (see Appendix).

"Hidden liabilities are fiscal time bombs aimed at future generations," warns Sid Taylor, research director of the NTU Foundation. "Many fiscal commitments and unfunded liabilities do not show up in the budget."

He adds that like the passengers on the *Titanic*, taxpayers are on a collision course with a red-ink iceberg. "Rearranging the deck chairs won't help," he says, "but fundamental spending reform will make for smoother sailing ahead."

The growth in the TLI, however, indicates that Uncle Sam is more interested in piling up liabilities for the next generation than guaranteeing their future.

A note of caution: If you hope to borrow money from some government agency, better do it quickly. At some point, even the manic U.S. Congress might realize that we are drowning in red ink and turn off the spigot.

M

17

Mass Transit

Brother, Can You Spare Train Fare?

If you've ever traveled from Manhattan to La Guardia Airport and back, you know the round-trip toll on the Triborough Bridge is $7, a hefty highwayman's extortion with almost no escape.

So you rationalize that it's okay because it goes to pay for the bridges.

That's absolutely untrue. One of the great lies of the twentieth and now the twenty-first centuries has been that the tolls are collected until the bridges and tunnels "are paid off." The trouble is that the bridges were paid off a generation ago.

In fact, in one recent year, these tolls—all part of New York's Triborough Bridge and Tunnel Authority—brought in a *profit* of $337 million! Does the money go to improve the roads for the car drivers who pay the bridge tolls? Nonsense. It mainly goes to subsidize the city's subway system (which won't get you to La Guardia) and the people who do *not drive*.

Americans love their cars, but Washington hates them. The federal government is desperately trying—unsuccessfully—to push us off the highways into mass transit, especially onto a giant new network of light-rail systems in major metropolitan areas.

The new lines are proliferating all over America, as railroads did a century ago. In the last twenty years, new commuter light mass-transit systems have been built or expanded in Washington, Los Angeles, San Francisco, Atlanta, Baltimore, Miami, Buffalo, Sacramento, San Diego, and Salt Lake City, with dozens more planned. But today they are being built at an exorbitant cost, generally double or triple their original estimates.

And there's another difference between now and the expansion one hundred years ago. Then, people flocked to the rails. Now, they mainly ignore them and continue to ride in their cars.

Who pays for these new mass-transit systems?

Naturally it is the car driver, just as his bridge tolls pay for the New York subway. It all comes out of the 18.4-cents-a-gallon federal gas tax. We've seen that some of that $20 billion a year is wasted on pork "demo" projects. We've also seen how up until 1998, more than a third of the gas tax went into everything from welfare to limos for government appointees. Now it's the straphangers' turn at the trough.

In one of the most wasteful boondoggles in American history, over $100 billion in gas-tax money has been invested over the years in the generally failed light-rail system. Now, through the newly passed $218 billion TEA-21 "highway" bill, another $42 billion is being spent on mass transportation that the masses of people don't want.

"The new train systems are being subsidized by Washington supposedly in order to decrease the congestion on the highways—to get people out of their cars into rail systems," says Wendell Cox, a transportation consultant who has testified before Congress several times. "But people prefer their cars, so with federal and local costs, we've wasted most of the $200 billion invested by Washington and localities so far. I'd say that overall, we've decreased road congestion by only one half of 1 percent through light rail construction—not a very impressive record for all the money we've spent."

Cox's studies indicate that after billions of dollars' worth of investment, the BART system in San Francisco, for example, has relieved road congestion in the area only by less than one day in a year, about the same result as in Saint Louis. The only system built in the last twenty years that has been mildly successful is the $8 billion money-losing Washington rail network, which has cut congestion by four days a year, still not a very impressive record.

The train systems have been robbing the local and federal pocketbooks as well. A ten-mile ride on a mass-transit system will cost all governments involved anywhere from $10 to $15, while a bus trip eats up only $3 in costs, as opposed to less than $1 in tax money for a car for the same trip.

The fantasy was that we could build a low-cost, high-ridership system. But that has never materialized. Rather than drop the dream, TEA-21 has increased the appropriation for mass transit by 20 percent. For mayors, it is found money, for the new systems have only one basic value—more trips to downtown. Otherwise, they are virtually useless in covering the suburban sprawl.

The dream was that people would leave their cars and take the train. *But exactly the opposite has taken place.* A recent study showed that train ridership is lower today than it was in the early 1960s when the mass-transit drive began.

In 1985 former senator William Proxmire (D., WI), the author of the Golden Fleece Award, presented it to the Urban Mass Transit Administration for its colossal waste. "The

UMTA," said Proxmire, "has played Santa Claus to the nation's cities," and as a result, the programs have been "a spectacular flop—the Edsel of federal programs. Taxpayers taken for a ride."

One side effect of pumping federal monies into mass transit has been a wild increase in costs. From 1970 to 1989, for instance, public transit cost rose 20 percent more than even inflationary health costs. In the first fifteen years, it rose 393 percent! Seventy percent of all federal subsidies have not been used for new rails, but just for those cost increases.

From 1945 to today, mass-transit ridership has dropped from 23.5 billion passenger miles to 7.5 billion, an enormous cut. And where it has risen slightly in some locales, the rise is not due to drivers abandoning their cars, but to a switch from low-cost buses to high-cost local trains—at four times the cost. In Portland, OR, whose light-rail system opened in 1987, most new riders were old bus riders.

Most new lines have overestimated ridership, only to become discouraged by the reality. Buffalo spent more than $600 million, mostly federal money, to construct a rail line, but the combined bus and rail ridership is much like the old bus ridership before the money was invested.

Miami's Metrorail, built in the 1980s with federal assistance and a final price tag of over $1 billion, is ridden by only 1 percent of Dade County residents—who still dearly love their cars.

There have been a few partial successes, but most are mainly failures of varying degrees. One superfailure has been the Los Angeles system, which has futilely tried to stem the tide of car travel. Because of severe financial difficulties, construction on two of the four remaining extensions of the Red Line has been suspended. The L.A. County Metropolitan Transportation Authority does not have the money to complete the line, whose additional cost is estimated at $6.1 billion. The reason? Mainly the lack of riders.

What are we going to do about the dilemma of light-rail passenger lines, their lack of riders, and their costs to taxpayers?

Will people eventually follow Big Brother's lead and drop their love of the automobile, which grants them total mobility, something the railroad cannot do?

No way. Not now, tomorrow, or ever.

So why is the federal government investing perhaps *a half trillion dollars eventually* to build rail systems most people don't want?

The answer to that is the answer to the dilemma of *unrepresentative* government that Americans face today. If we had the right Initiative and Referendum (see Part Three), would we approve this massive, unending boondoggle?

I would venture an emphatic "No!"

What to do?

- Save the $42 billion appropriated for mass transit in the new TEA-21 bill.

- Reduce the gas tax by 20 percent, limiting its use only to highway construction.

- Cancel the federal plans for new rail systems. If localities want them, let them pay for it.

- Continue to expand the highway system so that Americans can enjoy the transit system *they* love— the great American car.

18

Merchant Marine

What Happened to Old Glory at Sea?

A recent television special about the burgeoning cruise business pointed out that among the 250-plus ships that ply the oceans for pleasure seekers, there was only *one* ship registered under the American flag. It sails in and around Hawaii, an American sanctuary to begin with.

Carnival Cruise Lines, which owns the Holland-American Line as well, does most of its business here as a public corporation traded on the New York Stock Exchange. But when it comes to registering their ships in the United States, they—like their competitors—race for the ocean. Instead, their giant fleet of cruise vessels *officially* calls Panama its home. Even the ships of all-American Disney are registered in the Bahamas, another substitute port of call.

That embarrassment to the U.S. economy and pride is nothing when compared to America's constantly declining maritime shipping business.

Even though we are the world's largest exporter, some $1 trillion a year in goods, half by sea, all the American-flagged *merchant ships that sail international waters account for less than 3 percent of the world's gross tonnage.*

The rest ship out on foreign-flagged vessels, even if the ships and cargoes are American-owned, which is often the case.

Why? What stupidity or banality scares ships away from bearing the American flag? What keeps us from being competitive in the world market?

The answer is simple: The U.S. government, the unions, and the shipping companies are all in a quiet agreement to hit up the taxpayer in subsidies, which have already cost us $10 billion since the 1930s. Through its archaic Maritime Administration and with the help of the U.S. Congress and its overregulation of the shipping industry, Uncle Sam is pushing—no, really shoving—the American merchant fleet toward extinction.

Under the guise of "helping," they have made ships that fly the American flag so expensive that they cannot compete in the world market.

Though America is the most vocal spokesman for a free-market global economy, and the enemy of state-controlled businesses, as in China and even in Japan, when it comes to the merchant marine (what little we have), they make those nations look open and free.

"If we fly the American flag, we have to follow government regulations, which include using Maritime Administration–licensed seamen and officers. We also have to ship our goods in American-built ships," explains an executive of one of the leading shipping companies. "It's getting harder and harder to do that because America is not building a single container ship at present. Our ships are getting old and we have to go to foreign shipbuilders. Besides, the wage scales of American-licensed seamen are way too high—about $80,000 a year for a regular seaman and $100,000 a year and up for an officer. Nonlicensed seamen get about half that. We can't compete at the present government-influenced pay scale, which is why, even though we're an American company, two thirds of our ships are foreign-flagged. That's how we escape most of the regulation of the Maritime Administration."

(Other estimates of mariner salaries run as high as $100,000 for a six-month-at-sea year.)

The government doesn't challenge the shipping executive's description. The General Accounting Office states:

"Most of the higher costs are crew costs. U.S. crews receive higher wages and other benefits, and U.S.-flag vessels have higher manning requirements . . . U.S. shipyards generally charge more to build and maintain vessels than foreign shipyards. As a result, U.S.-flag vessels generally have higher capital and maintenance costs."

That's an understatement. U.S. government control is much greater than anything we see in other businesses. When it comes to the merchant marine, it sometimes seems like a conspiracy to destroy the fleet—the victory of bad politics over common sense.

America now has only 349 privately owned ships flying Old Glory. That's down twenty-two ships just from 1994 to 1998, and dropping. One government estimate is that it will be only 215 ships by the year 2002. Worse yet, more than 20 are inactive, about 50 are chartered by the Defense Department, 134 are in domestic trade. Only 165 U.S.-flagged ships are engaged in international shipping—carrying only 3 to 4 percent of the world's ocean-borne cargo.

Why? Because they couldn't make any money flying our flag.

The "conspiracy" starts out by limiting the number of seamen who are licensed. Then working with the unions, the wages are kept so outlandishly high that the industry avoids Maritime Administration oversight.

The government has a noose around the industry's neck. Under the Jones Act of 1920, only U.S.-built, U.S.-crewed, U.S.-flagged vessels can operate between U.S. ports, such as from New York to Miami. The result? Cargo traffic is cut way down. These ships are so costly that there's not a single coastal freighter bigger than one thousand tons (a small cargo vessel) working the East Coast. Indeed, turkey farmers in the Carolinas buy more expensive Canadian grain, shipped here on Canadian ships, rather than use the cheaper U.S. feed brought in by expensive American ships.

The whole bizarre system cuts down on farm exports overseas and even purchase of American food in the coastal states. Naturally, and correctly, farm-state politicians such as Senator Charles E. Grassley of Iowa want to cut out the subsidies.

In addition, the proviso that the ships be American-built and American-maintained makes no sense. If a U.S. merchant ship gets repaired in a foreign port, where costs are much lower, they have to pay a 50 percent tariff to the American government. Worse yet, most of the U.S. fleet is old, within a handful of years from extinction, and there are no competitive shipyards in America in which to build new ones. The shipping companies would have to bear the higher capital costs of new ships, which they won't do.

Worse yet, much of the American fleet is still steam-powered, as if Robert Fulton were running the Maritime Administration. Meanwhile, almost all foreign ships are diesel-powered, making them more efficient and able to use less fuel.

Then why are *any* ships U.S.-flagged? Because Congress bribes them—with a small fortune of your taxpayer money.

Only one of the many subsidies for the maritime industry is the Maritime Security Program. Begun in 1996 by Congress, it subsidizes forty-seven privately owned ships a year at the rate of $2.1 million each so they can fly the flag and pay the exorbitant mariner wages. In return for the $100 million a year, these ships promise to convert to government use—at a price—in case of national emergency.

The hole in that theory is that the Defense Department has an entire fleet of 215 ships, mostly in mothballs, which can be used in any emergency. In addition, they already charter almost 50 civilian ships.

To get the American flag hoisted on a container ship, Washington also bribes them by giving them enormous subsidies to carry cargo overseas for the government. This is called "preference cargo," and the law requires that overseas shipments by the armed forces, the Department of Agriculture, the Agency for International Development, and others be made on American-built, American-manned, American-maintained, American-flagged ships.

How much extra does that cost the taxpayer? About $50 million a year?

Try $710 million a year, the figure that federal auditors have come up with, making these shipments *double* the cost of normal international charges.

Has this giant bribe helped?

Apparently not. Says one government auditor: "Historically, cargo preference laws have not prevented a decline in the share of ocean-borne cargo carried by U.S.-flagged vessels."

Our laws keep the U.S. merchant marine barely alive as an antique, overly expensive, noncompetitive operation. With Maritime Administration costs, training of seamen, and other charges, including a $121 million "operating subsidy," still being phased out, it all sets us taxpayers back about $1 billion a year.

It would be worth it if it helped to revive the merchant

marine and make it competitive with foreign carriers who now carry most of *our exports* overseas. But the opposite appears to be true.

So what's the solution to this ridiculous, self-defeating situation?

It's a harsh one, but probably the only way:

- Cut out *all* subsidies to the maritime business.

- Have the Defense Department maintain its merchant fleet in mothballs and activate it in case of a national emergency.

- Stop the government-union conspiracy that keeps the salaries of a few thousand seamen at a ridiculously high level.

- Close down the requirement that the ships be American-built. Under present conditions, that's pragmatically impossible.

- If all else fails, close down the Maritime Administration itself and let the free market rule. That still allows the competent Coast Guard to do its work, whether on American or foreign-flagged vessels.

You'd be surprised by the results of true competition.

Perhaps someday you'll be able to take a cruise to the Caribbean or Europe, lean back on a chaise lounge, then look up from the sports deck and watch Old Glory flapping proudly in the breeze.

19

Metric System

How Many Millimeters Long Is Your Foot?

The following questions should be easy—if you're French.

- How tall are you—in meters and centimeters?
- How much do you weigh—in kilograms and grams?
- How fast does your Ford Taurus go—in kilometers per hour?
- How hot is it outside, now that it's twenty-five degrees Celsius?
- How many milliliters in that glass of milk?

You don't know? Naturally. Neither do I. Nor do I care.

But we should know and care, says the United States Congress and the Department of Commerce—and they've been spending millions of our tax dollars to get us hooked, metrically speaking.

Not only that, but they've set up a federal mandate with several pieces of legislature to try to *permanently* obliterate all the standbys of the hundreds-of-years-old American system. They're spending your money—$5 million worth just since 1993—to get rid of our revered measurements of *pounds, inches, feet, ounces, miles, Fahrenheit, quarts, yards, acres, and what have you.*

And substitute what? Naturally, the international metric system of centimeters and milliliters and kilograms and centigrade and other foreign measurements. Government officials are determined to thrust it down our throats, but if public opinion is any guide, American citizens are quite happy with the old system, thank you.

It all began in 1875, in Sèvres, France, when America signed the Treaty of the Meter, which established the International Bureau of Weights and Measures. Treaty after treaty followed, supposedly obligating America to conform to world standards. In 1893 metric systems for length and mass were *supposedly* adopted in America. The customary measurements of foot, pound, and quart were defined in relation to the meter, kilogram, and liter.

But that, of course, was all on paper. Almost no one, except for some scientists, paid any attention. Washington is still 248 *miles* from New York; the average American male is five *feet* nine *inches* tall and weighs about 155 *pounds*. The temperature in the summer hovers around 75 to 80 degrees *Fahrenheit*.

Washington is not 397 *kilometers* from New York. Men are not 1.753 *meters*, or 175.3 *centimeters*, tall, and don't weigh 70.3 *kilograms*. At least not the last time I looked.

But in 1968 the U.S. government got serious about pushing us stubborn Americans into the metric system. A forty-five-person panel advised the U.S. Department of Commerce that the conversion to the metric system should be adopted quickly, calling their report: "A Metric America: A Decision Whose Time Has Come."

In 1975 Congress passed the Metric Conversion Act and established the U.S. Metric Board. But by 1982 the public said the time had not come and the Board was disestablished. But the metric lobby did not quit. It came back with the "Omnibus Trade and Competitiveness Act of 1988," which called the metric system the "preferred system of weights and measures for United States trade and commerce."

By law, federal agencies were required, with certain exceptions, to use the metric system in their procurements, grants, and other business-related activities by the end of 1992. A 1991 Presidential Order by George Bush reinforced the legislation.

Though smaller, the campaign by Washington is still going on, pushed by the Department of Commerce through a program called "Toward a Metric America."

And their budget has been going up, not down, since 1995.

The biggest push has been on highway signs. *In fact, the Federal Highway Administration developed a metric conversion timetable for all of America. They planned to change the present signs—including speed limits, distances, and mileposts—to kilometers by September 30, 1996.*

All states that received federal money (all fifty of them) had to comply. Or else.

When the notice was posted on the Federal Register, comments were invited. The response was overwhelmingly negative—2,288 no's out of 2,731 answers. Aside from the fact they just didn't like it, many cited the waste of money. Each sign change was estimated at $70. The government claims there are six million highway signs, which is probably underestimated. But even at that number, the cost would be $420 million. That does not include the mileposts, of which there are millions upon millions more.

So the harried metric people posted a notice in 1994 that

the 1996 deadline was *temporarily* waived. But the state of Alabama decided to go ahead on its own.

In the winter of 1996–1997, they began a *total* switch from miles to kilometers, and actually redid a good part of the state. The howl from citizens could be heard from Birmingham to Montgomery. "What in the hell is a kilometer?" outraged citizens complained, some pointing out they were thinking in miles anyway.

"The whole program lasted about nine months," says an Alabama state spokesman. "We had to change all the kilometer signs back to miles, which cost extra money."

There are a few things that Americans do tolerate in the metric system. For example, soda is often sold in *liters*. Americans go along, but that's only because a liter is almost the same measure as a quart. Vitamins have always been sold in milligrams and micrograms, which is why we have no idea how much is in the bottle.

The metric program, which is being run by the National Institutes of Science and Technology of the Commerce Department, is even after the homemaker. They've published a recipe sheet for "Metric Chocolate Chip Cookies," and one called "Metric in the Kitchen," showing a 250-milliliter pot and a 50-milliliter "cup." Few cooks seem impressed, or even know what they're talking about.

Washington is a stubborn propagandist and they insist they're going to convert us all to metric. I doubt it—as long as Americans continue to face down the government, as they've done in this case.

The solution: CLOSE DOWN THE METRIC OPERATION, now and permanently, and save the money we would use for conversion.

Besides, nobody is going to tell me I weigh 80 *kilos!*

20

National Parks
Purple Mountain Majesty and Red Ink

Americans love their national parks, all 376 of them in forty-nine states and the District of Columbia, all eighty-five million acres, from the old standbys of Yosemite, Yellowstone, and Grand Teton, to such relatively new ones as Tallgrass National Prairie Preserve in Kansas.

They love them so much that they make three hundred million visits a year to tread their forests, streams, and mountains—sometimes to the point of overflowing. Not long ago, Yosemite had to close down certain facilities because of the overload of seekers of its nature and beauty.

Congress and the executive branch should be congratulated over the years for creating and supporting the national parks with a $1.6 billion annual budget, a number that rises 5 percent a year in the hope of solving the myriad problems of the parks.

What is their major problem?

Mismanagement and waste, sometimes of an incredible nature, by the federal government, a responsibility that falls on both the bureaucracy of the National Park Service (NPS) and that of the Congress, which has passed several illogical bills that now hinder the managers.

Together they must shoulder the blame for tainting the magnificence of our federal splendor in the West.

It seems that the parks are deteriorating before our eyes, with a backlog of maintenance of roads, bridges, drainage, etc., that is reaching crisis proportions. A federal audit indicates that it will cost some $4 billion to fix the infrastructure of the parks, which have sixteen thousand permanent structures, eight thousand miles of roads, fifteen hundred bridges and tunnels, five thousand housing units, and over four hundred dams. One federal report showed a bridge at the Acadia National Park where the mortar was coming out of the joints, and dangerous road-bank erosion at Rocky Mountain National Park.

That crisis has been made worse by the mismanagement of the Park Service.

First, the NPS has been wasting money in construction, paying out about 50 percent more than they should. At a congressional hearing, the Interior's inspector general testified that housing near Yosemite that cost the NPS $584,000 per house could have been built in the private sector for $250,000! Other housing at the Grand Canyon that cost NPS $390,000 should have come in at $158,000 less.

Even more serious is evidence that the NPS is wasting some $50 million a year through simple bad business.

A perfect example is the ridiculous contract the National Park Service draws up with the 655 concessionaires who sell the visitors everything from soda pop to lodging to meals. Is that a small business? Judge for yourself. Most recently, the concessions took in $714 million from the public, a figure that will reach a billion dollars in a few years.

But did the parks get their fair share of the money?

Absolutely not. Of 555 contracts examined, concessionaires took in $135 million, of which Uncle Sam received a franchise fee of only $3.6 million, or less than 3 percent of the gross.

Is that a sign of bad management? Absolutely. In contrast, other concessions in the federal government did *three times* better, with franchise fees that averaged 9 percent. That meant that for every $11 of sales, most of Uncle Sam's agencies received an average of $1. A few agencies, such as Veterans Affairs and Transportation, took in about a 25 percent average, or close to $3 for each $11 in sales.

And what of the national park concessions—stores, lodges, souvenir stands, etc.? Uncle Sam received a pitiful *thirty-five cents*, leaving $10.65 for the concessionaire.

Why?

The culprit here is legislation dating back to the Concessions Act of 1965, which gave concessions *priority* privilege for a new contract once theirs expired, say in twenty years. Because of that entrenched position, competition is scared away from bidding, which can be an expensive proposition. The apparently spineless National Park Service feels it must make a deal—generally at less than 3 percent. If the NPS received a reasonable 10 percent franchise fee, it would mean $71 million in their coffers each year, money that could be used to restore the damaged infrastructure.

What's worse is that the NPS doesn't even get the money. The franchise fees, as small as they are, go directly into the U.S. Treasury in Washington, more apt to be used for a congressional whip's $40,000-a-year snacks than to fix a single bridge and enhance the majesty of the parks.

Everyone loves the national parks and wants to protect them. But what can we do when we're outflanked by bureaucrats and Congress? The answer:

1. Tell your congressmen you want new legislation mandating a 10 percent government cut for all concessions in all national parks. This can be implemented as new contracts come up, as they do regularly. Tell concessionaires: take it or leave it. Take my word for it, they'll take it.

2. We need new legislation mandating that all the franchise fee money goes *directly* to NPS for exclusive use in upgrading the deteriorating infrastructure.

The *real* problem is the government culture that makes everything that's easy seem so complex—like looking at the beauty of the parks through smoked glasses.

Of course, we all hope the concession laws are changed in favor of the government. But if not, I've got a hot dog stand for you with a mountain as a backdrop where you can keep ninety-seven cents on every dollar you collect.

Now, where else can you get a deal like that?

21

Native Americans

Gambling Casinos: Revenge on the Palefaces

If you notice, I'm being politically correct using the term "Native Americans" even though the government calls it the Bureau of *Indian* Affairs.

The plight of the American Indian, who originally occupied this blessed land, is well known. To help make amends, the Bureau has a $1.7 billion budget, but that's not the only agency helping Native Americans. A study undertaken for me revealed that thirteen different federal agencies are spending another $3 billion a year, with little positive effect.

The Native American population of two million, which is growing rapidly, is still America's poorest, with excessive unemployment, low life expectancy, and insufficient education. Overall, it is another classic case history in the failure of large-scale federal social programs.

In addition, the entire Washington/Native American effort is rife with inefficiency and corruption. The General Accounting Office studied Indian Trust Funds, which included $2.1 billion for 314 tribes and another $453 million for individual

Indian accounts, money from oil, gas, and coal leases and investment income.

What did they learn?

That the books were, to say the least, in a muddle. They found that the monies could not be financially reconciled. After five years of work and millions in costs, they said that "a total of $2.4 billion for 32,901 receipt and disbursement transactions could not be traced . . ." adding that "the account owners will have no assurance that trust fund balances are accurate."

One of the gravest problems in the Indian/Washington welfare state is the failure of their housing program. Forty percent of Native Americans on the reservations live in over-crowded or inadequate housing, compared with 6 percent in the overall U.S. population.

Of the two million Indians, 1.2 million live in reservations or in nearby counties, most on "federal trust lands." The land is supposedly theirs, but it is actually held in "trust" by Washington. Forty-five million acres are in trust for the tribes, and ten million for individual Native Americans.

Banks are naturally reluctant to grant Native Americans mortgages—knowing that reclaiming the house in case of default would be difficult, if not impossible. (Native American land cannot usually be transferred to non-Native Americans.)

The result is that *only ninety-one* conventional mortgages were granted Indians on trust lands in a recent four-year period, almost all in only two tribes and by two banks. In 1996 Washington passed the Native American Housing Assistance and Self-Determination Act, which authorizes HUD block grants to tribes and increases leased-land limits from twenty-five to fifty years. But the GAO believes the bill's value is "uncertain," especially since banks still don't want to take trust land as collateral.

So the building of houses for Native Americans again

reverts to the welfare state, with all its stupidity and inefficiency. How stupid? How inefficient? How corrupt?

You judge.

"The Bureau of Indian Affairs' Portland area office had not provided decent, safe, and sanitary housing to eligible Indian families, and over 51 percent of the costs reviewed had been spent improperly," says the inspector general for the Interior, which is the agency responsible for Native Americans.

The IG goes on to say that forty-six of the individuals who received government-subsidized homes were ineligible for the housing and that construction prices were inflated by $226,000.

Virtually the same was true in Sacramento, where over 68 percent of the costs were spent improperly. Of $2.2 million in payment for houses for Indians, $522,000 was for inflated prices and services never provided.

As the inspector general of HUD recently told Congress, "the Native American housing problem is reaching crisis proportions."

But the biggest exposé of corruption in Indian housing came not from the IG or the GAO, but from a daily newspaper. In a six-month investigation of Indian housing in the Northwest, the *Seattle Times* turned up information that surprised even government investigators inured to the waste in federal programs.

The paper found that a few tribal insiders were benefiting from squandered millions in federal housing funds, while most Native Americans continued to live in squalor.

The *Times* learned, among other things, that:

- Just north of Everett, Washington, a 5,300-square-foot house worth $400,000—without the land— was built with federal HUD money earmarked for low-income Indians. The owner was the head of the tribe's housing authority, who, with a spouse, had a joint income of $92,000.

- In Tokeland, Washington, part of a $1.2 million HUD grant was used to build a large home for the tribal chairman.

- In Lapwai, Idaho, a $1.8 million HUD grant was used to build four large houses that no one on the reservation could afford to rent.

So if the welfare state has failed miserably to help the American Indians, does that mean that there is no hope?

Absolutely not. There's a new path opening, and it's called *capitalism*. It's coming to the reservation as GAMBLING, or gaming, as Washington likes to call it, and it's truly big business. It may be not only the savior of the original Americans, but their ultimate revenge against the palefaces who took their land.

How much do we owe the Native Americans? How much is America worth? If we assume an $9 trillion annual domestic gross product, and figure value at fifteen times cash flow, the country is worth $135 trillion. We don't expect to pay the Indians back that much, but if the casinos continue to expand, we'll make a sizable dent in the debt, one chip at a time.

But why Indians and gambling? The gimmick is simple. The courts have decided that the Native American tribes are "sovereign." As a result of treaties with the U.S. government, they have powers on their reservations not granted to ordinary citizens. So, although Connecticut does not allow casino gambling for others, it permits, even encourages, the two very successful Indian casinos—the Mohegan Sun and Foxwoods, the nation's best-known Indian gambling operation.

Native Americans now operate 281 gambling facilities, run by 184 different tribes in twenty-six states. Some tribes are as small as two hundred people, others as large as tens of thousands. As of last count, they take in some $7 billion a year from gambling and bring home about $2.5 billion in net cash, more than the budget of the Bureau of Indian Affairs. (And because they are Native Americans, there are no federal or state taxes on tribal earnings.)

The handsome vigorish was, however, a little lopsided. Half the money went to ten tribes, and some thirty tribes didn't make a nickel. A couple of casinos have even gone broke, and a few are in debt.

Some of the big winners are the Mashantucket Pequot Tribe of only a few hundred Indians in Connecticut who run the fabled Foxwoods; Mohegan Sun in Connecticut, operated by the Mohegan tribes, who have about one thousand members; the Shakopee, a Sioux tribe in the outskirts of Minneapolis; the Oneida in Wisconsin, not far from Green Bay; and the Seminoles in Florida, who run four operations, including ones outside Miami and Tampa that cater to tourists with bulging wallets.

The secret, of course, is to be close to a large concentration of palefaces, eager to contribute their cash to once-oppressed Native Americans.

Most of the gambling net goes to the tribe for housing, roads, education, and other communal purposes. But in some instances, individual members actually get a personal check in the mail. Just a few years ago, the Shakopee sent out checks to their small tribe, enriched by the palefaces of Minneapolis.

How large a check? A thousand dollars, perhaps?

Try *almost a half million a person, or $2 million for a family of four!*

With that kind of capitalist results, and with a little management help for less-successful tribes, we might someday make the Indians self-sufficient capitalists.

So what should we do?

Let's divert more of the $588 billion in gambling we throw away each year, and move it to the Indian casinos. What difference does it make where we lose the money? This way, maybe the Native Americans will get rich enough so we can forget about the Bureau of Indian Affairs, HUD, and the $5 billion a year in tax money we now spend on Native Americans.

Meanwhile you might have heard that President Clinton's great-grandmother was ostensibly one-quarter Indian. So why not do a little genealogical checking yourself? You never know. You might also become eligible to get an Indian gambling check in the mail.

That would be the paleface's ultimate revenge against tax-crazy Washington.

O

22

Outhouses

Relief Is Just a Fortune Away

Remember the $640 military toilet seats?

For a long while they were wonderful symbols of how Washington cavalierly flushes away our money. Now the National Park Service has taken toilets one step further in the world of fiscal irresponsibility.

This not only involves toilet seats but actual commodes put under a single roof in a two-seater outhouse.

Built in the Delaware Water Gap National Recreation Area, ninety miles north of Philadelphia, the commode was designed to give relief to hikers in their time of need.

So what's the problem? What could an outhouse possibly cost?

National Park officials didn't dwell on that question as they designed a unit of extraordinary proportions. First, the building has no running water, so you can't wash your hands afterward—or before. Nor can you flush the toilets. Instead, they installed a special composting variety of high-tech quality that cost $3,000 each.

They're also the most durable outhouses ever constructed. A typical home has a foundation that is six inches thick, but park officials were apparently worried about an earthquake in that nonearthquake area, so they built a foundation for the out-house *twenty-nine inches, or two feet five inches, thick.*

The building was surrounded on three sides by porches, but there was no place to sit down. The gabled roof was made of the finest slate, and the building base is of cobblestones. Inside, the baseboards are painted with a $78-a-gallon custom-mixed evergreen-hemlock-colored epoxy resin that matches the sur-rounding woods.

The design is exceptional for an outhouse, but it should be. The design work alone cost $102,614. When it was all done, depending on whom you ask, the final cost of the outhouse was either $330,000 or $445,000, a world record for a two-seater. This is in an area where a home with two thousand square feet of space, three bedrooms, and two baths sells for $110,000.

When the Philadelphia Inquirer *asked an official at the National Park Service about the cost, they were told: "Frankly, that's what we're paying for toilets."*

This outhouse will always be famous for its cost and design, but it's mainly important in understanding the philoso-phy of the American government. As a National Park official pointed out: "We could have built it cheaper, but we wanted someone coming up the trail or off the road to encounter a nice rest-room facility."

So much for roughing it in the federal wonderland.

P

23

Peanuts

Want to Buy Some Bootleg Nuts?

Every time you bite into a Snickers bar, or serve your kids peanut butter, or gobble a bag of Planters while watching television—think about this:

Your government is charging you $500 million a year extra in order to cozy up to peanut farmers who are living off their fatty crop. (Remember former President Jimmy Carter, who made his fortune in Georgia peanuts.)

By ignoring their own rhetoric about a free market, the government is rigging the peanut business by setting an inflated support price of $610 a ton, almost twice that of the world market.

Do you have an empty piece of land? How would you like to get in on this racket and make money raising peanuts with almost no risk?

Sorry, but you can't unless you have a federal license— what the Department of Agriculture calls a "peanut quota." And you can't get one anyway.

If you try to pull off a peanut deal, watch out for the feds.

It's like making moonshine in the mountains, or rum-running in the old days of Prohibition. If you think that as a free American you can grow and sell whatever you want on your property, think again. Strange as it may seem, the raising and selling of edible peanuts for the domestic market without a quota is illegal!

(See U.S. Code, Title 7, Section 1359A.)

The peanut sheller or "handler" who puts "nonquota" peanuts into the domestic food market pays 140 percent of the price as a penalty. The government can collect by placing a lien on everything he owns, including his house. The peanut farmer who falsifies his peanuts as "quota" when they're "nonquota" can even be criminally prosecuted by the government for fraud.

What's going on? Why threaten citizens for the sake of the lowly peanut?

It's all part of an archaic government program whose key is the "quota," the license to farm domestic peanuts, which only thirty-three thousand people hold. It was first issued to struggling farmers during the Great Depression. But peanut farmers are not struggling anymore. With that piece of paper, the government decides how many peanuts they can grow for domestic consumption in order to keep up the artificially inflated price, pleasing a handful of people with friends in Congress.

They're not handing out those licenses anymore, so the paper itself has assumed great value, much like the medallion of a New York City cab.

Only one third of the quota owners actually farm peanuts. Mostly, those who inherited the paper from their pappies now sell or lease their quota to other farmers at exorbitant rates. They collect an estimated $200 million a year, which further raises the cost of the peanuts we eat.

The racket is foolproof, even if it's patently unconstitutional. By permitting only quota owners to sell into the domestic edible peanut market, the Department of Agriculture can limit the size of the crop, which is now worth $1 billion. They can push the domestic price of a ton of nuts to $610, or higher, no matter how low the world price.

The current price is closer to $640 a ton while the world market is $350. That's one reason Americans are eating fewer peanuts.

Can you get into the racket by playing around with peanuts in your backyard? Yes, the law allows you to raise domestic edible peanuts on *one acre* without a quota. But Washington is shrewd. The cost of such a small crop will be larger than your income.

Does the scheme at least include farmers all over the country? Hardly. Forty-five percent of quotas are in a few counties in Georgia, and another thirteen percent are in Texas. The concentration of this legal racket in a few hands is even greater. Eighty percent of the peanut quota is owned by only 20 percent of the growers.

All this restraint of freedom has bothered some legislators, especially in the North, where more voters eat peanut butter than raise peanuts. In the 1996 Farm Bill, Senator Rick Santorum of Pennsylvania managed to cut the price support down from $670 to the present $610—which is still almost double the real price if there were no quotas.

In the House, Congressman Chris Shays (R., CT) worked to defeat the entire peanut program in the 1996 Farm Bill and came within three votes of victory. But the quota rolls on.

The price of peanuts is rigged so high that the "peanut marketing associations" set up by the Commodity Credit Corporation, the federal agency that loans out money to peanut farmers, not only don't suffer losses, but actually make a profit.

Recently they sent out a dividend check of $53 million to Georgia peanut farmers—money earned only because the gov-

*ernment rigs the peanut prices, and forces you to pay for it as
a consumer.*

The next time you eat a peanut butter sandwich, think
about why we tolerate this restraint of everyone's right to farm
what they want without a government license.

You might also consider the megabucks eaten up by this
bizarre program: the $500 million in the inflated price of
peanuts we eat; the $200 million the quota owners pick up
from those who actually farm the peanuts; and the $20–$50
million peanut crop insurance paid by the government.

What is the solution to this shell game?

1. A nonquota farmer should sue the USDA and take his case
    to the Supreme Court, which *must* side with him and rule
    the whole peanut racket unconstitutional.

2. A few smart politicians—outside of Georgia and Texas—
    could get together and sponsor legislation to eliminate the
    entire program, posthaste. It's an embarrassment to decent
    government.

Meanwhile, don't look now, but I've got a large bag of
bootleg peanuts for sale at half the rigged government price.

Any takers?

24

Pork

$15 Billion a Year to Study Why Politicians Are Compulsive Spenders

A grant of $107,000 to study the sex life of the Japanese quail.

That was my favorite item in the first *Government Racket* compendium of pork. I can't say that I can top it, but there seems to be no end to the nonsensical waste of our money emanating from the enormous Washington sausage machine.

One of the great joys—and pains—of researching government waste, ignorance, and chicanery is to catalog their padding of the budget to please constituents with dollars for pork, right out of the barrel.

Or at least to please those constituents who fail to understand that since almost *all* congressmen are porkmeisters, the little fat they receive is minuscule when compared to the massive nationwide rip-off of taxpayers' money.

In reality, of course, your congressman is not really bringing home the bacon, but just recirculating your tax money—*after* Washington takes its 40 percent vigorish. And too often, the part returned to you in pork is for some unneeded, even ridiculous, program.

But at least we can get a good laugh (or cry) at how our money—an estimated $15 billion a year—is being spent blatantly, with no conscience, apology, or remorse.

The pork is voted by Congress in thirteen different appropriations bills, but the money is actually spent by the executive branch. *In the great majority of the cases, the agency didn't even ask for the money.*

Every agency is involved in porkery by the Congress. The Department of Agriculture gets money for research, some of it trivial, such as the Japanese quail study. But it adds up to billions. The Department of Transportation is an enormous offender, witness "demonstration projects" (see Chapter 7). The Department of Defense is also a favorite vehicle for porkers. Even the National Science Foundation likes to waste money on "behavioral science" pork, while the National Endowment for the Humanities is the source of some misguided pseudoacademic studies.

In fact, there are three federal programs that are mainly there to provide pork of every description for members of Congress in virtually every district of the nation. The "pork agencies" include the Appalachian Regional Commission (covering twelve states); the Community Development Block Grant, a $4 billion rip-off that covers communities in 80 percent of the nation, including such affluent ones as Greenwich, Connecticut (which recently turned down its federal grant); and the relatively new Economic Development Initiatives (EDI), a euphemism for the infamous HUD Special Purpose Grants, which are also nationwide.

One of the big sins of pork is that most of the projects go to the districts and states of the members of the House and Senate Appropriations Committees, denying a "free lunch" to other taxpayers, who get only the drippings. In effect, pork is a cunning *fraud* perpetrated on the mass of the American people.

Check out these items for governmental fat of every nature.

The list looks exhaustive, but it actually represents only a *minuscule* portion of the pork that gets placed on the taxpayers' plate every year. And please note that while some of the waste is obvious, other projects are packaged with high-sounding titles that disguise that the federal money is misplaced.

- $104,055 to study how people communicate through facial expressions.

- $77,826 for "Coping With Change in Czechoslovakia."

- $300,000 for a "History of Electrification in Portland, Oregon."

- $5 million to Montana State University for a conference on underused natural resources.

- $76,971 to study "Human Responses to Repeated Floods." (Victims get depressed and move to higher land.)

- $1 million for the eradication of brown tree snakes.

- $125,000 to compile a "Sino-Tibetan Etymological Dictionary and Thesaurus."

- $100,000 to preserve a Revolutionary War gunboat at the bottom of Lake Champlain, which was named, then unnamed, by Congress, as the sixth Great Lake.

- $400,000 to study "The Expressive Culture of the San Blas Islands" in Panama.

- $19.6 million for the International Fund for Ireland, which started as a going-away gift for Speaker Tip O'Neill and which funds many items, including golf videos and pony centers on the Old Sod.

- $100,000 for the Alaska Gold Rush Centennial Task Force.

- $300,000 for "whirling disease" research at Montana State University (that state again).

- Funds for seventy workers in the Bureau of the Census to count the population of Bangladesh and 225 other countries.

- $5 million for a new Parliament building in the Solomon Islands. Problem is that it's part of the British Commonwealth.

- $1 million Utah study on how to cross the street.

- $600,000 for the restoration of the Sotterly Plantation in South Carolina.

- $200,000 for the Don Henley Caddo Lake Institute in Colorado.

- $1.13 million to maintain historical notes at the College of Physicians in Philadelphia.

- $90,000 to study the social life—not the diet or health—of vegetarians.

- $1 million for the rehabilitation of the John Hay estate in New Hampshire.

- $500,000 for the University of Hawaii Center on the Family.

- $160,000 to compile "The Atlas of Historical County Boundaries."

- $4.8 million for a child development center at Camp Pendleton Marine Corps Base.

- $5 million for King County (Washington) park-and-ride lots.

- $875,000 for the Franklin County (Massachusetts) traveler information system.

- $1.25 million for the Montana World Trade Center (Again?).

- $140,000 to count the Samoan population of Orange County, California.

- $3.45 million for eight EDI projects in Pennsylvania, including $700,000 for a fitness center in Lehigh Valley.

- $384,000 for a federally paid census of the cats and dogs in Ventura County, California.

- $400,000 for the renovation of a theater by the Eureka Coal Heritage Foundation in Indiana.

- $1 million for "community development" in LeClede Town, Saint Louis, Missouri.

- $50,000 for the town of Wellston, Missouri, to fix up its town hall.

- $3 million to fix the Fifth Street bridge in Highland, Missouri.

- $2 million for "environmental education" in Highland.

- $1.5 million for infrastructure needs at the Apple Valley Science and Technology Center in Missouri.

- $491,607 for a party to honor nine hundred employees of the Department of Agriculture—a saving over the previous year's bash, which cost $667,000.

- $105,000 to write a "History of American Communes, 1965–75."

- $1.35 million for the renovation of the Paramount Theater in Rutland, Vermont.

- $1.2 million to replace the lobby marble, plus $600,000 for new Italian-designed desks, for the European Bank for Reconstruction and Development, which gets $70 million a year from U.S. taxpayers.

- $109 million for new federal loans to students who had already defaulted on their old loans.

- $5 million in antipoverty funds for an interest-free loan to Sears, Roebuck.

- $4 million for a new columbarium at the National Memorial Center of Arizona.

- Funds for gifts of Rolex watches to contractor employees, paid for by the Environmental Protection Agency.

- Millions spent by the Agency for International Development in Miami and New York to convince American businesses to move out of the United States and relocate in Latin America.

- $20,000 for three marble elevator floors in Congress.

- $3.22 million for updating the Scarborough Library at Shepherd College in West Virginia, home of Senator Robert Byrd, the King of Pork, once chairman of the Senate Appropriations Committee, and now its ranking (minority) member.

- $1.5 million for the renovation of theaters in Manhattan, obviously a poor American town.

- $1.5 million for another intermodal transportation center, this one for the Geyserville (California) Visitors Center.

- $60,000 to study "Labor Activism in the Soviet Union, 1918–1929."

- $900,000 to restore a German U505 submarine at the Museum of Science and Industry in Chicago.

- $100,000 in federal funds to connect a private mobile home park to a Minnesota city water supply.

- $13 million for a National Swine Research Center even though thirteen different federal facilities are doing the same work.

- $3.1 million to create a "Housing Futures Institute" at Ball State University in Indiana.

- $15 million for the preservation of antiquities—in Egypt.

- $12 million for a study entitled "Towards Other Planetary Systems."

- $2 million for the Walk on the Mountain skyway so that tourists can view nearby Mount Rainier. The problem is that the mountain is usually visible only one out of six days.

- $14,000 to study "Depictions of Daily Life in the East German Cinema, 1965–66."

- A $227,000 National Science Foundation study of what people find funny, including off-color jokes.

- $1 million to demolish the Casey Hotel in Scranton, Pennsylvania.

- $5.4 million for the Hawaii Small Business Center.

- $393 million for the Natchez Trace State Parkway in Tennessee, a project of the Appalachian Regional Commission—"a road to nowhere." An Interior Department official laments that it is a nice road, but such a shame that nobody uses it.

- $119 million for a three-story Visitors Center at Hoover Dam that was originally budgeted for $32 million.

- $2.5 million to restore a railroad station in Thurmond, West Virginia. One problem: The town has a population of eight residents.

- $750,000 for a Graveyard of the Atlantic Museum for shipwrecks on Hatteras Island, North Carolina.

- $300,000 to find the Confederate submarine H. L. *Huntley*, which sank after successfully attacking the U.S.S. *Housatonic*. (A federal fascination with wrecks?)

- $600,000 for Aztec ruins in New Mexico.

- $300,000 for the National First Ladies' Library.

- $300,000 for the transcription for the oral history of Iowa labor unions.

- $6 million for the Robert J. Dole Institute on the campus of the University of Kansas. (Consolation prize for the 1996 election?)

- $1 million for the Paul Simon Public Policy Institute at Southern Illinois University. (Another former senator gets his gift.)

- $5,100,000 for a child development center at Fort Irwin, California.

- $4.3 million to tear down 19 naval radio towers near the Naval Academy in Maryland to preserve the "natural setting" for rabbits and deer.

- $500,000 for a "water taxi" in Savannah, Georgia.

- $475,000 for the Women's World Cup of Soccer.

- $350,000 to enhance the cultural awareness of Saint Louis.

- $3 million for leaking fuel tanks in rural Alaska.

- $1 million for a Center for Early Southern Life in Huntsville, Alabama.

- $500,000 to improve the site tipple and yard at the Lackawanna County Coal Mine. (What is "tipple"?)

- $500,000 to renovate the Opera House in Enosberg, Vermont.

- $250,000 for a National Soccer Activity Center.

- $450,000 for the Institute of Software Research in Fairmont, California. (Shouldn't Bill Gates pay for this?)

- $1 million for an enlarged chemistry department at Wittenberg University in Ohio. (What about my alma mater?)

- $250,000 for the renovation of the Westhampton Beach Performing Arts Center, Long Island, in one of the richest towns in America.

- $300,000 for the design study for a National Museum of American Music honoring Frank Sinatra.

- $229,460 to study the sex life of houseflies.

- $2.8 million for a Louisiana school of cosmetology to cover the tuition of 673 students. But only 19 got state licenses, at a cost to taxpayers of $148,000 per.

- $129,000 to create a database of Gregorian chants.

ENOUGH? BUT PLEASE DON'T ASK ME TO STOP NOW.

- $161,913 to study "Israeli Reactions to Scud Attacks During the Gulf War." (They were frightened.)

- $1,708,696 to prevent "conduct disorders" in children, a project on which parents have spent five thousand years and over a trillion dollars—with no results.

- $10.4 million for a physical fitness center at the Bremerton Puget Sound Naval Shipyard even though there are five gyms within a five-minute drive.

- $183,000 to the University of Georgia to measure differences in self-esteem among people.

- $172,000 grant to researchers at Cornell University to learn how strongly people feel remorse.

- $15 million for debt retirement (pay off old bills) for the Port of Portland, Oregon.

- $9,720,625 more for the Jacksonville (Florida) "Automated Skyway" extension, a project that has cost $34 million per mile—about twenty times the cost of regular highways. One DOT official calls it an expensive "amusement ride."

- $6 million for a communications network at the Indian Hills Community College in Iowa.

- $246,000 for the Toledo Farmer's Market to make it easier for residents to find bargains.

- $2.7 million for an Animal Resources Wing at South Dakota State University. (Who needs private donations when you have Uncle Sucker?)

- $85,000 grant to the American Bar Association to hold one hundred conversations on law-based democratic society (at $200 an hour?).

- $4 million for a gambling impact study. Answer: people lose money.

- $3 million for the Indiana University School of Medicine, the alma mater of the then-chairman of a House Subcommittee on Appropriations.

- $2.3 million for the William Howard Taft National Historic Site.

- $60,000 to an NPR (National Public Radio) station in Los Angeles to examine the local car culture by holding thirteen town meetings during drive time.

- $3.1 million for the National Writing Project. (Am I eligible?)

- $3 million for the Pell Institute of International Relations.

- $3 million for the Edmund S. Muskie Foundation.

- $5 million for the Central City streetcar in Portland, Oregon.

- $5.5 million for buses for the Salt Lake City 2002 Winter Olympics.

- $125,000 for a summer program for ten Maine teachers at $12,500 per teacher, to "study the role of photography in forming an American identity."

- $5 million for 2002 Winter Olympics "Intermodal Centers," the latest pork gimmick of the Transportation committees (see Chapter 7, Demonstration Projects).

- $2 million for buses in Syracuse, New York. (Under this principle, shouldn't Washington pay for buses in every city?)

- $15,000 for a series of radio conversations on "Appalachian Pluralism and Identity."

- $500,000 for the Van Emmons Population Marketing Analysis Center in Pennsylvania.

- $124,910 to find ways to reduce "school phobia." (Declare regular recess.)

- A grant of $2.5 million to the city of Carbondale, Pennsylvania.

- $19,275 for discussions on "The Role of the Press in the Public Life of America."

- $5.2 million for construction of the Indiana Center for Interdisciplinary Research and Education at Indiana State University.

- $105,163 to research the "Evolution of Monogamy in a Biparental Rodent." (Does this rival the sex life of the Japanese quail?)

- $2.6 million for the (Mark) Hatfield Marine Science Center.

- $14,000 to study "Deadbeats, Drunkers, and Dreamers: The Problem of Failure in the United States, 1819–93."

- $1 million for the construction of the Mystic (Connecticut) Seaport Maritime Education Center.

- $30 million more for research on electric vehicles, which has now received $75 million for work that should be sponsored by the auto companies. Toyota is already marketing a combined electric-gas car.

- $23 million to find out how long it takes mail to be delivered. (Too long.)

- $15 million for a footbridge from New Jersey to Ellis Island, where a ferry now services the visitors.

- $800,000 for the Delaware Gap National Recreation Area, enough money to pay for two more outhouses (see Chapter 22).

- $936,000 to the Palmer Chiropractor School in Iowa to conduct demonstrations for the public.

- $750,000 for the renovation of the Ryan Library at Iona College in New Rochelle, New York. (What about the other three thousand college libraries?)

- $220,000 to a Boston professor to study why (if true) women smile more than men. Perhaps because men pay more taxes.

(The sources are many, but special thanks go to the pork exposé specialists, Citizens Against Government Waste and the National Taxpayers Union, who are constantly fighting an uphill battle against porkers.)

The orgy of pork is expensive and changes little from year to year despite false rhetoric about saving money.

It can only be stopped by House and Senate resolutions that recognize that it is an immoral reelection device that takes advantage of unsophisticated voters who don't understand the gimmick.

But it can be stopped, with the following mechanism:

1. Much of this pork evolves in "conferences," added *after either the House or the Senate has voted to put in their not-so-little favors. Abolish the "Conference Pork Racket."*

2. All Congress has to do is pass a rule, in both the House and the Senate, that no member of any of the twenty-six Appropriations Committees can insert any *extra* funds for his district or his state in any of the appropriations.

3. To avoid "swapping" (I'll put one in for you, and you put one in for me), the resolutions shall define this as illegal behavior and police it with the threat of expulsion from Congress.

Citizens should bombard their members with letters, faxes, telegrams, Mailgrams, and e-mail demanding the end of pork, and using the $15 billion a year involved to *truly* reduce either taxes or the federal debt.

It's fun to read about pork (and it's fun to dig it up), but it's no fun when April 15 rolls around and we have to pay for this nonsense.

Q

25

Quakes, Hurricanes, FEMA, and Other Disasters

We Insure Everything

I was lecturing aboard a cruise ship soon after the Northridge earthquake in Southern California when I struck up a conversation with a guest from the area.

When I pointed out that Washington was putting a fortune into emergency relief, his eyes lit up.

"I live in Los Angeles and was home at the time of the earthquake in January 1994. One day I got a check in the mail for $3,000 from the government to pay for damage to my house. The funny thing is that not only don't I need the money, but I never applied for it. It just came."

Despite this hint of Washington gone astray one more time, the idea of disaster relief for emergencies is a good one. The federal government has helped out in Hurricane Andrew in 1992, the Great Midwest Flood of 1993, and the Northridge earthquake in the Los Angeles area in 1994, plus several hurricanes and floods since.

The relief money, which has averaged $3 billion a year recently, is part of the President's Disaster Relief Fund, and is administered by FEMA, the Federal Emergency Management Agency. Despite the high expenditures by FEMA—some $25 billion in the last decade—few of us know what the agency does and whether they, in traditional Washington fashion, waste a great deal of money.

There is, however, one person who does know, and that's the inspector general of FEMA, who has issued periodic reports on money spent when it shouldn't have been spent.

The theory behind the relief is to provide for essential services and to bring people back somewhat from the edge. But one area that's gray in the law, but quite green in FEMA, is the $286 million that has been spent in the nonessential arena of "recreational relief." Try this list:

- In Miami, the Dinner Key Marina, home of many luxury vessels, received $3 million to repair this "essential" operation after storm damage.

- Since everyone, including the White House, loves baseball, FEMA spent $5.6 million to repair the Anaheim Angels' scoreboard after an earthquake.

- At the Indian Wells Golf Resort in California, to repair erosion, cart paths, and sprinklers, FEMA came to golfers' rescue with $871,977 of your money.

- On the New Jersey shore there's a town called Loch Arbor, one of the smallest in America—five hundred feet long with only four hundred residents. A storm damaged their Beach Club building, but not for long. FEMA gave them $320,000—about $800 for each family in the town—to put it back into shape.

- Key Biscayne, Florida, was hit by one of its classic storms, which ripped up a lot of trees. FEMA gave their Crandon Park $3.5 *million* to replace trees, but it turns out that half the money was used to plant trees on their roads—not related to the park. Officials defended the move by saying the trees planted on road medians provided a posthurricane "psychological boost."

- FEMA paid $88 million to fix up the obsolescent Los Angeles Coliseum after earthquake damage.

- Damage to a golf course's fairways and greens brought in $246,102 from a concerned FEMA. Which course? Naturally, the Palm Springs Golf Course, part of an obviously needy community.

- Back in New Jersey, the Atlantic Highlands Marina was smart enough to insure their buildings and equipment. After a bad storm, they had $4 million in damage, some of which was collected from the insurance company. But they hadn't insured the piers and promenade. Who picked up that tab? The naive, ignorant, abused taxpayer.

One of the strangest aspects of the disaster waste is that the government covers losses not just for public property, but since 1970, for *private* nonprofit organizations, most of which are far from essential:

- A contemporary dance studio received $120,000 from FEMA to repair earthquake damage to its building.

- A performing arts theater received *$1.5 million* for damage from an earthquake. Why did they receive such generosity from Uncle Sam? Because they offered discount tickets to senior citizens!

- A religious retreat center for youth, which was also open to other religions, got $4.8 million from FEMA for earthquake damage—money for which they didn't have to pray.

Since FEMA is a government operation, its boondoggles take on unprecedented forms of waste. One of them involves public facilities that had been leased to the private sector, but received FEMA disaster cash anyway.

Examples abound:

- The Gilroy, California, Old City Hall is now a private restaurant and meeting facility. After the 1989 earthquake, FEMA gave $2 million to fix up the building.
- Pier 45 in San Francisco is leased out to a private fish-processing company. FEMA paid $9 million to repair the facility so that the vendors could stay in business with no obligation to Washington, or the need to carry insurance.
- The Port of Oakland operates thirty ship berths leased to private companies. FEMA paid millions to repair the berths.

One glaring example of FEMA waste is the Cypress Viaduct, a large overpass that collapsed during the 1989 earthquake in the San Francisco area.

At the time, FEMA estimated a repair cost of $360 million, of which Washington would pay 90 percent. The outcome? The project has cost the federal taxpayers over a billion dollars, and ten years later, it is just being completed.

The cost of FEMA expenditures (in addition to its yearly

budget of $300 million-plus to pay for twenty-five hundred salaries) in the past decade has been $25 billion. But that's only part of the disaster equation, an operation that includes the U.S. Army Corps of Engineers, HUD, the Federal Highway Administration, the Farm Service Agency of the Department of Agriculture, the Small Business Administration, and others. All told, that collective, often duplicating activity adds billions to the disaster bill.

FEMA needs an overhaul, including:

1. More audits by the inspector general.
2. Tighter definition of what is a disaster. The White House now labels twice as many incidents as disasters as it did a decade ago.
3. Eliminate compensation for any recreational activities.
4. Eliminate FEMA cash for any private operation.
5. Cut our payments for damage to public facilities leased to private businesses. Require the lessee to have full insurance coverage.
6. Eliminate the maddening duplication of disaster relief and put it all under one agency, perhaps FEMA—if they can get their act together and stop being a disaster on their own.

R

26

Radio Ads

Are We Paying to Pollute the Airwaves?

"This is your congressman, Representative Thadeus J. Public, and I'm talking to you over WPER radio, right smack in the middle of Jamie Jason's talk show.

"About what? A town hall meeting, that's what. It's going to be at the Jefferson Middle School—right over the railroad crossing and turn right at Saint Bart's Church. When? Well, at seven-thirty P.M. tomorrow night, and it's all about a problem facing all of us—how the federal government can make elementary education work in our district. I'm going to be doing the speaking, and you can ask the questions. Now, I'm reading from the red-covered regulation book from the Franking Commission. It tells me I have to say the following to my radio audience:

"This is all paid for by official funds authorized by the House of Representatives."

What's going on? A radio ad by a congressman paid for by the taxpayers? How come?

Sounds bizarre, which it is, but it's quite legitimate, if not particularly nice for taxpayers. These radio ads are not part of the members' official reelection campaign, which would be paid for by contributors. No, this is just one more way to keep his name—and now his voice—in front of the public through an extension (read "loophole") of the franking law, which also pays for the congressional members' postage.

With this relatively new perk, which few voters know about, any member of Congress can go beyond the cost of the "newsletters" he mails to constituents to supposedly let them know what goes on in Washington. He can now announce his own self-promoting town hall meeting through radio ads as well as place advertisements in the local papers. The tab for all of this comes out of his office money, what is called the MRA, the member's representational allowance, which is now about $1 million per member per year.

The theory is that with the town hall meeting, he's "educating" the citizens. But all sensible people—in and out of Washington—know that's just an expensive sham that allows congressmen to run for reelection *continually*, one reason that 93 percent are returned to office. He can do it around the calendar for his two-year term, except for the ninety days before election.

How much can they spend on these radio and newspaper ads? I asked the bipartisan Franking Commission.

"As much as the congressman wants," they responded. "These radio ads come out of his MRA, and are not controlled by the office limit on postage." One former congressman, Steve Stockman (R., TX), spent $68,800 on radio ads to let people know he was around.

The member of Congress also hits us up for the cost of the meeting, a gimmick that can be much more expensive than the ads to draw a crowd. The Franking Commission guidebook explains exactly what they can spend your money on to shape up a town hall meeting:

- Transcription of what's said at the event
- Audiovisual expenses, such as making a videotape of the meeting
- Electronic transmission, getting it on radio and television
- Rental of rooms and chairs
- Public address system
- Interpreting services (in case many people speak, say, Spanish or Chinese)
- Signs, banners, leaflets, flyers

All this hoopla is typical during campaigns, when *outside* money is paying the bill. But in this perk, it's me and you who are supporting what is in effect campaign publicity for an elected official we may not vote for.

What to do?

First, Congress should eliminate the first perk—radio and print advertising for town hall meetings.

Second, Congress should curtail the second perk—government-paid town hall meetings themselves. We hear and see enough of our congressmen on radio and television.

If our representative wants still more publicity, the mother's milk of politics, he can always go on Jamie Jason's radio call-in talk show.

He'll reach more people, and the price for taxpayers is just right.

Nothing.

27

Recording Studios

High Tech—in Your Face

Ever see a U.S. senator or representative on television, seated behind a desk with the American flag at his side, making an impassioned speech about a piece of legislation he is sponsoring?

Of course. And we all assume that he is in the studio of a network, or in some local television station in Milwaukee or Atlanta, or anywhere, where the cost of the operation is being picked up by the station.

But you may be wrong.

Instead, the senator—or House member—may be in an elaborate, state-of-the-art government recording studio on Capitol Hill having it all done on videotape. The studio is able to feed to cable stations all over the nation through live satellite broadcast, and can put the member on radio anywhere in the country with modern digital phone lines.

Or they can record him or her on video or audiotape and send it out anywhere in the nation—bringing the member's face and voice right into your home whether you want it there or not.

Who then picks up the tab for this electronic marvel, another of the great perks for our perk-happy congresspeople? Naturally, you the watcher—the American taxpayer. When it comes to government, this is the closest thing to pay TV, but one you didn't dial in.

There are not one, but two, subsidized recording studios in Congress. The Senate Recording Studio is located in the basement of the Capitol, and the House Recording Studio is in the basement of the Rayburn House Office building. Together they are eating up a small fortune in staff and equipment in order to publicize federal officeholders—who get a lot of free time on the air anyway without tapping into Uncle Sam's treasury.

In fact, there's a wonderful perk synergy for members of Congress. Those paid radio ads to push their town hall meetings (see Chapter 26, Radio Ads) can be recorded in the member's own voice right in the government recording studio.

What are they allowed to talk about on Government Air? Officially, it's "official business," which includes his "opinion" on an issue, or anything that adds to "constituency awareness"—meaning anything at all. What it does, of course, is add to the member's name recognition. Meanwhile his opponent goes scratching for exposure without the taxpayer-paid propaganda machine behind him.

The way it works is typical of government. The amount they charge members of Congress for radio and television video production, editing, tapes, and transmission, as we shall see, is only a pittance, made to look as if the members are actually paying for it out of their office allowance.

Both studios keep a price list, but absolutely *refused* to give it out. When it comes to congressional perks, they are paranoid to an extreme, trying to cover their collective tracks. It took weeks of calling, asking, then demanding the price list, only to be turned down by several possible sources. Finally a person on the staff of a reform-minded congressman—who shall not be revealed lest they seek vengeance against the turncoat—supplied it.

What's the budget for the studios? I asked that next, even going to the Senate's sergeant at arms, which is in charge of their studio. Again they refused to reveal this top-secret figure. Actually, it's easier to get the CIA budget—some $31 billion—than anything connected to the House and Senate recording studios.

I did glean a few bits of black-box information. One leak confirmed that the House alone has sixteen people working full-time on this electronic publicity mill.

Next I approached the House Budget Committee. A member of the staff tried everything, but even he couldn't find the total cost of this congressional publicity machine. "It's not listed anywhere," he told me after an exhaustive search. "It's buried in some other appropriation."

Why the *omertà*, the blood pledge of secrecy?

"I guess," he ventured, "because Congress will be faced with public outrage if people knew how much they're actually spending on providing radio and television recording services for members."

So can I guess as to the cost? The House staffer did have a piece of information to add to the puzzle. House members paid $264,000 last year to the subsidized studio to pay for their portion of the cost—which is probably one fifth the actual amount if they went to a regular outside studio. That would mean, conservatively, that with salaries, modern electronic equipment, and two studios, we're talking about $3 million a year to support this superperk.

Back to the price list. It's really an unsubtle joke, one of many pulled by Washington on the naive taxpayer. For making a fifteen-minute videotape production of a member seated at a desk with the American flag, the House studio charges members *all of $50* for the production, plus—and this is truly black humor—$10 for a TelePrompTer and $5 for titles, names, etc.

I called two studios in my area for comparative prices. They ranged from $500 to $3,000. The cheaper of the two studios I called, for example, charges a minimum of $100 for the TelePrompTer versus the House's $10.

Who makes up the rest? Naturally, as always, we do.

What should we do to save some money and cut down on Washington-disseminated propaganda?

There are numerous electronic media *eager* to put members of Congress on radio and television, either network or locally, any time they want, free of charge.

So?

1. Raise the prices so that congressmen will have to pay for their propaganda programs in full.

2. Have them pay for it out of their own pockets.

3. Combine the two studios into one and save a small fortune in pointless duplication.

4. Or just close down the whole operation, and cruelly push our members of Congress into the open publicity market. I assume they'll thrive nicely without the taxpayer's help.

Of course, eliminating congressional perks is probably harder to accomplish than winning the Cold War.

And remember, that took us forty-five years.

S

28

Small-Business Criminals
Holding Up Uncle Sam

Increasingly, the idea of a Small Business Administration makes less and less sense. In a recent year they guaranteed $9.46 billion of taxpayer money in bank loans for 45,288 *ostensibly* small businesses—out of a universe of twenty-five million. That's about one sixth of 1 percent of such enterprises, not even enough for the tail to wag the business dog.

Supposedly, these are mainly people who can't get loans elsewhere, which, as we'll see, is a product of Beltway imagination.

But that aside, a new wrinkle in government stupidity has emerged from that agency, one that easily tops many a misguided operation reported in these pages:

The SBA loans multimillions of dollars of your money to criminals.

Who says so? The inspector general of the SBA himself. The report came as a result of "Operation Clean Sweep," conducted by the IG along with the Secret Service of the Treasury Department, the same people who guard the president.

It found that in a sample of 3,352 defaulted SBA borrowers

nationwide, one in eight had criminal records! In fact, they had committed still another fraud when they applied, claiming they had never been found guilty of a crime.

The case histories were a little chilling. The roster of "businessman" to whom the SBA gave your money even included a murderer. Try out this sample of how the underworld taps into our tax money:

- **One SBA borrower who got a $700,000 loan had a prior record that included five arrests for passing bad checks and resisting arrest.**

- **A borrower who had a long record of extortion and the sexual assault of a child was readily given a $47,600 loan.**

- **One crook with a nine-page criminal history of assault and weapons violations was graciously given $100,000 by the accommodating SBA.**

- **A $100, 000 loan was made to a man who was convicted of possession of stolen property.**

Sound ridiculous? Doesn't the SBA check their applicants for a criminal record?

Incredibly, no. All the crooked applicant has to do is *state* that he has no criminal record. "Under current SBA procedures," says the IG, "loan applicants who answer negatively to criminal-history questions are not subject to further criminal-record checks prior to loan approval. Their denials are accepted as fact."

The SBA *used to* make a criminal check of applicants through the FBI, which called on their criminal-history and name-check files to investigate. But in 1987 the FBI announced that it would do complete investigations only if it received the fingerprints of the applicants. Otherwise it would continue only manual name checks.

Apparently the SBA was outraged at the thought that *their* businessmen should have to be fingerprinted. They refused the FBI request. In fact, the SBA was also annoyed that the FBI name check could take thirty days or more, which slowed down their lending process. They canceled that as well. To look active and to justify their existence—and poor record—they needed to make as many loans as possible, whether the applicants were good citizens and would pay the loans back or not.

Are we talking about small change stolen by SBA criminal clients?

Apparently not. In just half the sample of defaulted loans from criminal borrowers, the loss was $33 million. Two other factors would make that figure even larger. No check was done of borrowers who did not yet default but might still have an unknown criminal record.

And those convicted of drunken driving, who lied on their applications, were not counted.

The whole fiasco of taking the word of criminals is an insult to good citizens, and not a particularly bright idea either.

The solution?

If you want Uncle Sam's money, you shouldn't be afraid to be fingerprinted. That should be compulsory—despite the Department of Justice's concerns about "privacy." If not, the FBI should be required to do a criminal-history check, which would turn up the great majority of crooks.

But before we leave the SBA, we should look at other problems of this agency, some of which I enumerated in my first edition of *The Government Racket.*

1. Though the agency's goal is to help borrowers who have been turned down by commercial banks, 60 percent of

applicants surveyed said they could have gotten the loans elsewhere without an SBA ironclad guarantee to the bank that the loans would be paid—by the borrower or by Uncle Sam.

2. The government's working definition of "small business" is humorous. A struggling building contractor with two employees would find it hard to get an SBA loan, probably refused for being too "small." In fact, the typical SBA loan is made to businesses with a million dollars gross annual revenue.

    Even that can be small potatoes in the government lexicon. "Businesses with revenues of $3.5 million, and in certain cases up to $14.5 million, may be considered small . . ." says a government report without a smile.

3. The SBA loves to loan money to well-to-do professionals who could borrow anywhere. In one two-year period they gave out some $450 million to 2,092 professionals, including doctors, dentists, and accountants, people who should not be on federal quasi welfare.

Despite giving money to people who don't need government guarantees, the SBA has a default rate five times that of regular banks. "Nonperforming loans" make up about 16 percent of the $43 billion portfolio, one reason the agency now costs taxpayers some $800 million a year. To that add the multibillion-dollar costs of defaults coming up over the years.

The solution? Easy. Since the SBA can help only a minuscule percentage of businesses, deals heavily in crooks—and loses a fortune in the process—there is only one possible solution.

Close it down and bank the money.

29

SSI—Supplemental Security Income

A Good Idea Too Often Gone Bad

In Georgia, a large family—perhaps best described as a clan—decided it would be cozy to live off the government. But how?

The easiest welfare program to scam in Washington is SSI, or Supplement Security Income, run by the Social Security Administration. It was designed to provide a floor income for the poor who were blind or disabled, or those aged whose Social Security check wasn't enough to live on—if they had that benefit at all.

A good idea, undoubtedly. But SSI, with its wide-open, almost bizarre framework, has become the warm, fuzzy home of cheaters, who come in an unlimited number of descriptions.

The Georgia family, which numbered a total of 300 people, was one of them. Of that group, 181—in four different generations—were receiving SSI checks from Washington each month. Investigators checked them out and found that one in three in the clan had faked their disabilities. Others had been "medically improved" but were still getting checks.

Overall, ninety—or half the family's SSI recipients—were

dropped from the rolls, but not before they had extracted $1 million in benefits from unsuspecting taxpayers.

For the poor blind, the aged without sufficient income, those who are schizophrenic and otherwise truly handicapped, the SSI is a lifesaver, even a life giver. Congress should be praised for passing the law, which grants the disabled and aged poor individual up to $494 a month, and $741 for couples. But our legislators should also be chastised for letting the program expand, even explode, exponentially without any sense, rhyme, or reason.

At the end of its first year, 1974, SSI had 3.2 million people on its rolls and cost the taxpayers a reasonable $3.8 billion. And today? There are 6.5 million recipients and the tab has grown to $28 billion, plus another $3 billion from the states!

That figure is larger than the amount AFDC (now called "Temporary Assistance for Needy Families") hands out in cash to mainly unmarried mothers and their children (see Chapter 34, Welfare).

Why? Has there been an epidemic of disabling accidents in the land? Have earthquakes taken such a drastic toll? Apparently not. The rise in rolls and cash is due—as the Georgia gang illustrates—to the program's enormous vulnerability to fraud and waste. It is, we should add, also a victim of traditional government stupidity.

Take children. The purpose of a disability pension is to make up for lost income, as in the case of a blind person who can't work. But children do not work, and usually do not earn any money. So why the "disability" pension for youngsters?

No one seems to know, except that there was a twenty-six-word provision in the original bill that has propelled the SSI children's program into multibillions of dollars. *In fact, a supposedly emotionally disturbed "hyperactive" child receives the*

*same, or larger, SSI monthly check from Washington as a truly
disabled male adult who cannot work to support his family.*

The growth in childhood SSI cases has been enormous,
even frightening. In 1989 there were 296,300 youngsters on the
disabled rolls. But by the end of 1994, that number had tripled.
By 1997 it had reached over a million, and the cost had reached
$5 billion a year.

Why? Is there a sudden medical epidemic affecting our children? Are they being run down by cars, or wantonly disabled in
hockey or Little League play? Hardly. The reason for the
growth is mainly loose government definitions of disability—
especially in the emotional area—plus a legion of parent-
scammers who take advantage of the taxpayers.

In Wisconsin, a father who was also on SSI taught his
daughter to put gum in her hair, act up in class, and get bad
grades. She was put on SSI as being mentally disturbed and
granted an $18,000 retroactive check. The family eagerly used
the money to buy a car and furniture, then vacationed in
Florida, all courtesy of Uncle Sam. A Kentucky parent used her
son's $13,000 back benefits for a car and a state-of-the-art
computer. Retroactive SSI payments for children have alone
cost the taxpayers over $3 billion.

In Illinois a mother and her three children, who were all
supposedly disabled, received $21,000 a year from SSI. Accord-
ing to the local school principal, it was all a sham. The youngsters went to regular classes and participated in routine
physical activities. SSI checks, the principal explained, were
known as "crazy money," because youngsters had to act crazy
to become eligible.

The biggest boom in fake childhood disability came after a
Supreme Court decision in 1990 in the case of *Sullivan v. Zebley,* which made it easier for children to qualify for SSI for

"mental" reasons. The new rules loosened the definition of "disability," giving it unscientific post-Freudian overtones. To become eligible, one needed to have a few of the following "symptoms":

- Mood swings
- Trouble sleeping
- Odd thinking
- Decreased energy
- Feelings of guilt or low self-esteem
- Or conversely, inflated self-esteem
- Inability to participate in age-appropriate activities

(By this definition, perhaps half the nation is "disabled.")

Combined with the "inability to function socially," and "inability to concentrate," these feelings made a child eligible for a $494 monthly SSI check.

Naturally, it was an invitation for fraud, a rush to collect Washington's "crazy money." Is it any wonder that an estimated half million children suddenly became "disabled" and joined the SSI roster? The result of the Zebley decision was to cost us an additional $5 billion.

The Welfare Reform Act of 1996 somewhat toughened the definition of childhood disability. According to an SSI official, 125,000 children have since been taken off the rolls. But there are still some 900,000 youngsters receiving $5 billion a year, legitimately or otherwise.

One of the most egregious *legal* scams in SSI history was the period, in the 1980s and part of the 1990s, when alcoholics and drug abusers were considered disabled. SSI graciously sent them regular monthly checks—including retroactive lump sums—so that they could pay for their habit. In 1983 there were 3,000 substance abusers on the rolls, a figure that rose magically to 160,000 by 1996.

The *Bakersfield Californian* reported on a woman who was arrested on charges of possession and use of heroin. During the raid the police found a paper sack with more than $5,000 in cash. Had she stolen it or gotten the money by dealing in drugs? the police asked. Absolutely not. The woman produced hard documentation that she had received $8,585 from SSI as back payment for her "disability" as a drug addict.

The public outcry forced Congress to amend the law. In 1994 they set a thirty-six-month SSI lifetime limit for substance abusers. Then in 1996, in the "Contract with America Advancement Act," Congress cut off SSI funds for those who were receiving benefits solely because of substance abuse. At the time there were 209,000 disabled abusers on both SSI and DI, the regular Social Security disability benefit for former workers.

Today, according to the House Human Resources Subcommittee, that number is down to 66,000 persons, saving us $1.2 billion a year. There are still abusers on the rolls, but supposedly only because they have other disabling symptoms.

The fight to eliminate substance abusers from SSI has mostly been won—a classic case of a public-versus-government struggle that taxpayers periodically have to make in order to restore a modicum of sanity to Washington.

The same SSI incompetence came to light when it was discovered that some jailed prisoners were still getting their SSI checks even though it is against the law. Sheriff Mike Grey of Butte County, California, heard rumors that some of his inmates were receiving SSI funds. He met with the manager of the local Social Security office. They compared notes and found that of Grey's 180 prisoners, 16 were still on the SSI dole. The inmates had even received $15,097 in overpayments!

The General Accounting Office has followed up with a study entitled "Efforts Fall Short in Correcting Erroneous Payments to Prisoners," which reported that loopholes in enforcement were keeping SSI checks coming to criminals across the nation. Studying the computer records of twelve large county and local jails, they learned that in just their sample, $5 million had erroneously been paid to 2,343 prisoners by SSI.

"Typically," says the GAO report with quiet cynicism, "the erroneous payment continued for 6 months or less and totalled about $1,700. SSI was unaware that many of these payments had occurred."

So how much is the total taxpayer tab for this prisoner scam? It's hard to compute, but the GAO says that SSI money went to some 4 percent of the prisoners. Since there are 1 million people incarcerated, it would mean that 60,000 prisoners are receiving SSI checks totaling some *$102 million* a year!

(The SSI disagrees with the GAO study, claiming that they catch 95 percent of the illegal payments to prisoners by comparing their rolls with the prison population. However, the GAO contests that disclaimer.)

There's still another hole in the SSI logic: its policy of paying out money to immigrants, especially aged immigrants. Supposedly they were vouched for by economically stable children who promised that their parents would not become public burdens.

Unfortunately, that's a lost goal, or a crooked pledge. Studies indicate that immigrants are twice as likely to receive welfare benefits as citizens. What often happens is that a well-to-do family sponsors their parents as immigrants, then simply denies their legal obligation. They "divest" their parents of their assets, what the SSI calls "deeming." After a three-year waiting period, the aged immigrant is eligible for SSI.

Were only a handful of aliens on SSI? Far from it. Their numbers totaled 825,000, and they cost us—as of today—some $4 billion a year.

After a public outcry, the Congress, on August 22, 1996, passed the Welfare Reform Act, which changed the law, but only temporarily. This act would have cut the alien SSI rolls down to 325,000. But in a compromise under the Balanced Budget Amendment of August 1997, all aliens who had been on the SSI roster in 1996 kept their benefits—never having been cut off to begin with. Today, new immigrants are not eligible for SSI, except in certain cases, but the alien rolls are up to 725,000 again.

SSI now spends $31 billion a year for all recipients (including $3 billion from the states), but apparently that's not enough. They are so eager to spend more that for years they gave "Outreach Demonstration Project" grants totaling $33 million to get new disabled and poor customers to sign up for SSI cash.

They did mass mailings, put up billboards, paid for radio and TV spots, held "benefit fairs," did door-to-door canvassing, and set up booths at state fairs. They even produced an SSI rap song enticing you to sign up for SSI.

But SSI wasn't all that successful at giving away your money. As they said, there was "the stigma of receiving public assistance," and "a reluctance to admit or accept disability as a permanent condition." They also had a problem, said SSI promoters, overcoming "Midwest pride." Two grantee employees in New Orleans were shot and others shunned because people suspected they worked for a local housing authority and wanted to raise their rents.

SSI workers were also shunned in Cambodian neighborhoods in Orange County, California, where Asian middlemen sign up immigrants by coaching them on how to lie and act disabled. They wanted no interference from Washington in their racket. Besides, it has been reported that 60 percent of Cambodian households have at least one member on SSI.

These promotion grants have been stopped, says an SSI spokesman. But to get new customers, they still use public-affairs advertising on radio and in newspapers, targeted heavily at senior citizens, along with posters that ask: "Do you know anybody with limited income who needs financial help?"

(If they're not careful, they'll find many ordinary citizens answering "Yes.")

SSI is becoming increasingly expensive, and is too burdened with waste and fraud.

Still other SSI scams have been enumerated by the government:

1. Some on SSI sent in false notices that they are separated from their spouse, in order to receive a larger monthly check.

2. Thousands of SSI recipients in nursing homes fail to tell SSI of their new home, and continue to receive their full SSI checks, which is against the law.

3. Middlemen who coach SSI applicants on how to appear to be disabled when they are not are costing the government millions. In one case a middleman was arrested for fraud after helping at least 240 people falsely obtain $7 million in SSI checks.

4. Despite the supposed tightening, hundreds of thousands of children are falsely receiving SSI disability checks for their behavior, which is sometimes coached to appear badly neurotic.

What can be done to cut down the $31 billion—and growing—cost of this open-ended entitlement program that spends whatever it decides it needs?

The solution is not too difficult:

1. *First, all children should be taken off the rolls.* Disabled children are no different from normal children economically. Few make any money. The inspector general of HHS, in looking at the program, concluded that SSI payments did not help prepare the children for a productive adult life.

   If there are some costs not covered by Medicaid that parents must lay out for disabled children, Congress should set up a small fund to handle that. But otherwise, the childhood disability eligibility for SSI should be discontinued by law. It makes absolutely no sense, and the savings will be over $4 billion a year.

2. The Social Security Administration, which handles SSI, does too little to curb fraud. Policing of SSI should be increased by setting up its own inspector general office and hiring inspectors.

3. In the case of the 725,000 aliens on the program, all should be required to apply to become citizens of the United States within one year after their eligibility period. If they do not comply, they should be cut out of SSI.

4. SSI's payments to prisoners should be reexamined by the GAO to see if correctional officials are complying.

5. Congress should reinvestigate the definition of disability, making sure that it relates to inability to work. Of the 6.5 million beneficiaries, there are probably a million or more who do not belong on SSI.

The savings? At least $10 billion a year.

Americans should never become mean-minded. But neither should they throw away good money.

For a true, total reform of our chaotic social welfare program—to create one that takes care of *all* the poor and disabled at a reasonable cost, with enormous savings in current duplicating programs—see Chapter 34, Welfare.

I believe you'll find it an eye-opener that transcends that hogwash of welfare ideologues on both sides of the political aisle.

30

Statistical Services

They've Got Our Number—Seventy-three Times

Want to know how many farmers there are? What the average manufacturing wage is? How long a fifty-year-old male can expect to live?

Is there one place in the federal government you can go to find out?

Silly. This is Washington. Duplication & Overlap is not a law firm but the standard government method of doing business.

Instead of one, there are *seventy-three* places you can go for answers.

The federal statistics system is not centralized. Instead it is spread out in seventy-three programs in fourteen different cabinet agencies and various independent agencies. In fact, the duplication is even greater than that. The audit that turned up those myriad "stat" services *did not count those that spent less than a half million a year!* The true number, which is surely well over one hundred, will probably never be known.

As an example of D & O in creating numbers for industry,

commerce, finance, labor, and health matters, there are *eleven* major statistical organizations handling the seventy-three programs. Together they spend $2.5 billion of taxpayer money to create salient figures.

According to the Office of Management and Budget, they include:

- Bureau of Transportation Statistics
- National Agricultural Statistical Service
- Bureau of Labor Statistics
- Bureau of Economic Analysis
- Energy Information Administration
- Internal Revenue Service Statistics of Income Division
- Economic Research Service
- Bureau of the Census
- National Center for Educational Statistics
- Bureau of Justice Statistics
- National Center for Health Statistics

The duplication is even worse than it appears. For example, in the Department of Health and Human Services there are *twenty-nine groups* doing statistical work.

There are many reasons this system is rife with inefficiency, even bias. Most programs report to political appointees, who may have ulterior motives in delivering certain numbers to Wall Street or the nation. Statistics, of course, can be wrong or twisted to sell a specific government story on inflation, manufacturing, labor costs, or whatever. The need for independence is vital.

So is the need for quality numbers. Recent debates on the

inflation statistics, which may be higher than Washington says, and cost-of-living figures, which may actually be lower, cast doubt on the results of the present crazy-quilt system. A major survey of professional statisticians showed that of the ten major industrial countries, the United States came out seventh in the quality of its numbers.

Does quality count? Absolutely, and it can cost us billions of dollars if the numbers are wrong.

According to The Heritage Foundation, research has shown that the government overestimation of housing inflation figures from the 1960s to the early 1980s resulted in a $50 billion larger deficit for fiscal year 1994 than it would have been if the figures were correct.

The CPI, the consumer price index, is another possibly false federal statistic that can come back to haunt us. The Congressional Budget Office estimates that if the CPI figures are too high by only one half of 1 percent, as experts suspect, then government spending—mostly on entitlements geared to inflation—would be $14 billion less by the year 2002.

In addition to better numbers, there is the need for lower cost in collecting the statistics. The present outlay of $2.5 billion a year is just too much money.

What can we do to get better numbers and save money in the process?

The answer is obvious.

We should eliminate all seventy-three statistical programs and set up one National Statistics Service that is independent of everyone.

The benefits are self-evident.

- **Independence eliminates political bias**
- **There is considerably less duplication**

- Overhead, which multiplies with each statistical program, will be reduced
- Better numbers
- Less manpower
- Greater coordination

The President should choose the head of a new centralized National Statistics Service, who will then be confirmed by the Senate. He or she should be a master statistician, unlike some other federal political appointees who, as they say on the street, "know from nothing."

The Service's first move should be to cut the total manpower in the former seventy-three groups and physically consolidate the offices into one, saving a fortune in overhead. How much saving overall? At least a billion dollars.

That stat is not much by government standards. But it still impresses the likes of you and me, who by this time should have figured out that Washington has our number.

T

31

Telephones

Just Charge It to Uncle Sam

How large is Uncle Sam's phone bill? And how much of it is waste?

Check out the annual report of most major corporations and you'll find the telecommunications costs in an instant generally as a subhead of their overhead.

But not the federal government. In its annual budget, Washington scrupulously avoids listing its total overhead, whether rent or telephone or salaries or pensions or benefits—or anything. Everything is broken down agency by agency, with no totals by function, a kind of backward accounting system designed to keep people like us from getting accurate numbers.

Then how much does Uncle Sam actually spend on the horn? And is it wisely spent, without much waste?

That was my mission, which turned out to be more difficult than I thought. Telephones and other communications—faxing, pagers, videoconferencing, etc.—are listed in the annual budget separately under each agency in a catch-all "Communications, Utilities and Miscellaneous Charges," which is Object

Classification No. 23.3. But the government makes it hard, perhaps impossible, to get the *total* amount of that category, let alone the true amount for telephones.

I did learn that the General Services Administration (GSA), as part of a program called FTS2000 (Federal Telecommunications Service 2000), contracts for telephones and other telecommunications for those government agencies that ask. Many do, but the agencies also reserve the right to buy telephone services on their own, which complicates the picture.

The GSA was very cooperative on their end. They provided me with their expenditures for several agencies. The winner was Defense, which spent $112 million a year on telephones through the GSA. On long distance, the GSA business is split between AT&T and Sprint, 75 percent to 25 percent. The prices aren't bad: six cents a minute.

The total of GSA long-distance calls for fiscal 1997 came to $681 million, from $23 million for Interior to the larger amount at Defense.

What about local calls?

GSA, which says it handles about 25 percent of the government's local telephone market, says they spent $243 million in 1997. That would make the government's total local phone business about a billion dollars.

To that, says the GSA, we have to add about $500 million for other telecommunications services such as faxes, data, videoconferencing, cellular, and paging services.

Thus far we have $1.65 billion, but we haven't learned how much agencies are spending on long-distance calling on their own. If we add $350 million, we have a round guesstimate of a $2 billion annual federal phone bill. Although they wouldn't commit themselves, the GSA people thought that was reasonable.

But I could never be sure.

The only place, they said, that I could get a final, accurate number was the OMB, the Office of Management and Budget. They, of course, should know *everything*, especially since they write the president's budget.

When I finally reached the OMB after four unreturned phone calls, I asked: "How much does the federal government spend on telephone calls?"

Their "Office of *Non*-Communications" never returned my calls after that. Apparently the real cost of government phone calls is a "black-box" secret much darker than any of the CIA's.

Meanwhile I had the $2 billion estimate. Next I had to learn if the money was being well spent. Was there much waste, fraud, and abuse involved?

Apparently, a great deal. The General Accounting Office (part of Congress) had studied the phone services of one agency, the Department of Agriculture.

Would that give me some insight into what actually goes on phone to phone in the federal government? Are they always talking business, or are the 1.9 million federal employees chatting away on our nickel (actually six cents a minute)?

I learned that the USDA uses—count them—*fifteen hundred* different commercial telephone companies. That's in addition to the General Services Administration's FTS2000. Agriculture, I learned, has 24,000 phone lines just in the Washington area, where, of course, they do no farming, except in the raising of our taxes.

What did the auditors learn? It seems that there is more fraud and abuse in the daily use of federal telephones than one would want—or expect.

For instance:

- They found that the USDA operators accepted and paid for inappropriate collect calls at least *half* the time. These included collect calls from 652 prisoners at eighteen correctional institutions! The USDA recipient of the call conspired with the prisoners, then placed other long-distance calls for them, billing it all to the government.

- USDA offices in Washington paid out tens of thousands of dollars each month for overseas calls without knowing whether they were authorized. (Bills were not checked.)

- Some of the overseas calls from Agriculture employees were to sexual "adult entertainment" numbers.

- The USDA did not monitor telephone credit cards supplied to employees.

- Hackers broke into USDA's telephone system and made an estimated $50,000 in international long-distance calls in just one weekend.

- A number of calls were made by employees to companies advertising jobs outside the government.

The auditors learned that the USDA was also wasting millions of dollars a year by:

1. Paying for unnecessary telecommunications services.

2. Leasing equipment that was not used.

3. Paying for services billed that were never provided.

4. Hiring commercial telephone carriers that charge up to three times as much as those in the GSA's FTS2000 program.

The problem is surely nationwide on a large scale in every federal agency. For instance, telephone hackers broke into the Drug Enforcement Administration (DEA) phone system and spent $2 million in calls over a period of eighteen months—mainly because the agency did not check its phone bills.

I learned that GSA had made three internal studies of their phone services. Could that give me a clue to the cost? I asked for copies, but they wouldn't release the inspector general's work without a Freedom of Information request. I reluctantly made the request—reluctantly because *all* that data should be public.

When the reports finally came in after almost a month, I found them hardly enlightening. *Every time the IG mentioned the cost of phone calls—which was why I used the Freedom of Information Act to begin with—the figure was blacked out.*

Why does the government treat the *real* phone bill as a closely guarded secret? Because the bureaucrats surely know what I was beginning to suspect—that the electronic "horn" is often a toy in the hands of federal employees.

The total cost of the telephones is still a secret. But there's one thing I can promise you. If it's the last thing I ever do, I'll find out the *real* phone bill of the U.S. government.

U

32

Universal Service Fund

Reach Out and Touch Someone—
Like Harrison Ford

What do you and I have in common with Harrison Ford—
except for the fact that we envy his good looks and extraordinary wealth? Simple. *All of us chip in—involuntarily—to pay
for his phone bill.*

By a twist of logic of which only Uncle Sam is capable, the
true cost of your telephone usage never appears on your bill.
Instead, the Federal Communications Commission has been
granted the right of taxation by Congress, which it then uses to
manipulate telephone costs to reward some people and punish
others. As John Berthoud, the head of National Taxpayers
Union, points out: taxation by unelected bureaucrats such as
the FCC is "undemocratic."

It is called the "Universal Service Fund," and its goal is to
provide phone service for everyone, including people in remote
areas—where the local phone company may have to spend a
great deal per line. So the USF, which takes its money from me
and you, gives *subsidies* to phone companies to beef up rural
telephone service.

How does the FCC get the money from us? In the form of higher phone bills.

So what does this have to do with Harrison Ford? Well, he has a giant western ranch, as do a dozen or more Hollywood luminaries, and even some Wall Street giants. Money is taken from regular phone users in cities, suburbs, and towns so that the FCC can give subsidies to the rural phone companies that service the well-heeled like Harrison Ford. In escaping regular civilization for his privacy, he becomes hard to reach. But it costs a lot to bring in and service such isolated phone lines, which is why our pockets, not our phones, are being tapped.

USF is no respecter of need. It can give to the rich, like Ford, or to any rural resident. According to Citizens for a Sound Economy, that subsidy—and several other connected to the Universal Service Fund—now cost over $3 billion a year, all of which is disguised by being "off-budget."

Take Bretton Woods, New Hampshire, for example. This town is a small affluent resort community near the Canadian border, famous for the 1944 treaty that set up the World Bank. The Bretton Woods Telephone Company handles only 491 phones. But it gets $18,000 a year from the FCC's Universal Service Fund, which means that we subsidize each subscriber to the tune of $37 a year!

The company was a small privately owned firm until 1992 when it was bought out by a large conglomerate—which means we're subsidizing not only wealthy phone users, but big corporations as well.

The whole subsidy system is lopsided. Long-distance phone users also kick in to pay for those who don't much call out of their area. If one looks at the long-distance phone advertisements, we would guess that ten to fifteen cents a minute is a "bargain." In actuality, long distance *should* be very cheap.

The government pays only six cents a minute to AT&T and

Sprint for their calls. Estimates of the real cost of long distance are as low as one cent a minute. So why do we pay so much? Because long-distance phoning includes a giant subsidy from our bills that is used to support local service. How much? Probably $1 billion or more a year.

The solution?

- **Eliminate subsidies from urban-suburban to rural phones, which can be just plain unfair—witness Harrison Ford and Bretton Woods.**

- **Eliminate subsidies from long-distance rates to local rates. There was a time when long distance was uncommon. Today, since it can mean as little as ten miles from your home, it is commonplace. Instead of ten to twenty cents a minute for a long-distance call, the real price should be no more than five cents, perhaps less. This could happen once the tax-payer subsidies are eliminated.**

In its infinite miscalculations, the government—in this case Congress and the FCC—is acting unwisely. These two phone subsidies, which make it easy to reach out and touch the wrong people, are a case in point.

Besides, can't Harrison Ford pay for his own phone line?

Come to think of it, why doesn't he just buy the local phone company and tell the taxpayers to forget the subsidy?

V

33

Volunteers (Americorps)

In Washington They Get Paid

In 1993 the White House retreaded an old idea under the slogan of "reinventing government." The program was basically a domestic peace corps, a group of young people who—as "volunteers"—would help clean up slums, fight drug addiction, do environmental work, and even help out in teaching. All noteworthy goals.

It was to be called "AmeriCorps," and to distance it from similar, but failed, Great Society programs, the White House promised that this one would be different.

The young volunteers would be under the umbrella of the Corporation for National Service, which would be run, they said, like "a big venture capital outfit, not like a bureaucracy"— implying it would be efficient, inexpensive, and not wasteful. In fact, said its promoters, it would be "a model enterprise, not just for government, but for many sectors of society."

This, of course, was from an enterprise (the U.S. government) that has become a master of manic promises and overoptimism as excuses for their often chronic failure of the truth.

The proposed original AmeriCorps budget was to be $7.4 billion over five years, and the staff was to number some hundred thousand youngsters. Congress cut that back to $1.5 billion for three years, with an actual budget of $442 million in 1998 and $516 million for 1999. Still not chicken liver, but enough to support twenty thousand spirited young people.

The unique aspect of the program was that it was to be a *volunteer* corps. Mind you, not the kind of real volunteers being promoted by General Colin Powell, who has helped marshal young and old to work *without pay* as part of America's eighty million volunteers.

AmeriCorps was unique. Their "volunteers" were to be paid. Not a fortune, of course—a mere $7.50 an hour, along with medical benefits, child care, and a $4,725 educational voucher on completion of their service.

So how expensive could that be for the U.S. Treasury?

We soon found out. Not long ago, their books were audited. It turns out that the *actual* annual cost of a "volunteer" in the Corps ranged from $25,797 to $31,017, depending on the project.

A cursory look at the personnel table for the federal government showed that the higher amount is more than the salaries for the bottom three grades of federal employment, GS-1, GS-2, and GS-3. In fact, the $28,500 mean cost of these "volunteers" is as high as the typical American wage.

In essence, the volunteer AmeriCorps had merely increased the size of the federal bureaucracy.

This "model" for America was designed as a "reinvented government" organization that would take only 5 percent of the total monies for overhead, the hallmark of a new type of Beltway activity. Did they meet the goal?

Hardly. *Unfortunately, it turned out that more than half the average expense per member went to overhead.*

A third of the monies spent by the AmeriCorps went into grants to other organizations. One of those was the Border Volunteer Corp. (BVC), established by the Arizona-Mexico Commission, which received $2.8 million from the corporation. It was audited by the inspector general, who found $189,458 in questionable expenditures:

- The executive director traveled four times to Mexico even though the work was to be solely in the United States.

- Salaries were excessive, and the director's salary of $86,194 was double that of the predecessor.

- BVC purchased a $12,000 car and paid commuting expenses for its comptroller.

- The staff routinely paid for meals and entertainment unrelated to travel status, etc.

A congressional committee looking into the AmeriCorps found that one of the grants, $2.9 million to the Northwest Service Academy, actually cost the government *$45,000* per graduating participant.

Many of the AmeriCorps projects were far off base. In Orange County, California, a branch revealed that while they were supposed to provide service for more than fifteen hundred people, none of the four programs ever had more than twenty-five participants, and most ranged from five to fifteen. In Denver some AmeriCorps members earned their "volunteer" money by handing out leaflets attacking a city councilman.

The new type of bureaucracy, which was supposed to be more like a venture capital company than a government operation, never materialized. Naturally.

Another audit of the National Service Corporation, including AmeriCorps, was performed by the accounting firms of Arthur Andersen and Williams, Adley & Co. It showed that not only had the NSC not "reinvented government," but that they were carrying on the grand tradition of federal mismanagement.

According to the accountants' report, the AmeriCorps lacked strong management controls; failed to maintain accurate information; lacked acceptable budgetary controls; presented unreliable and inconsistent financial statements.

The idea of paying "volunteers" was a bad one to begin with. Corruption and waste soon reared their slovenly heads. The overhead was too high and the management raggedy.

What then should we do with this costly pseudovolunteer operation?

Simple. Volunteerism is a people's, not a governmental, arena. Paying volunteers destroys the power of the social contract and tarnishes both its participants and its goals.

Therefore, we should:

- **Close down the AmeriCorps and save the remaining $50 million.**

Most important, let's encourage the former AmeriCorps kids to get real jobs in the private sector. Then they can truly *volunteer*, without pay or the trumpeting of Washington propaganda, for any one of many worthy charitable causes.

W

34

Welfare

It's Bigger Than You Think

Conventional wisdom, which circulates like hot air, is that welfare in America is a *small* item in the federal budget. In fact, so say seers, now with "welfare reform," it is even smaller, maybe infinitesimal. In all, it is often laughed off as small potatoes, some 1 percent of the federal budget.

In reality, this is one of Washington's great lies of all time.

When people say "welfare," they envision unmarried women with children receiving checks in the mail. The reality, as we shall see, is that this program, which used to be called Aid to Families with Dependent Children (AFDC), is fiscally the puniest of our enormous welfare costs.

In my appearance before a congressional committee handling the oversight of welfare, I started by reading from a virtually unknown 226-page catalog of federal welfare programs.

I read the opening paragraph with as little emotion as possible:

"Almost 80 benefits programs provide cash and noncash aid that is directed primarily to persons with limited income.

These benefits programs cost $367.7 billion in Fiscal Year 1996 . . . Federal funds provided 71.1 percent of the total and *welfare* [emphasis mine] accounted for 16.7 percent of the FY 1996 federal budget."

What? Almost 17 percent of the budget?

As I read it I shocked most of the congressmen on the panel. They were listening to numbers that had never been presented to them before. *The federal-outlay part of that $368 billion welfare outlay was larger than the entire defense budget, making welfare the largest spending item in the government!*

Plus, of course, another $107 billion in welfare from the states.

So much for that innocent, ridiculous *1 percent* gossip.

The welfare catalog I was reading from, entitled "Cash and Noncash Benefits for Persons with Limited Income," was actually produced by the Congressional Research Service, a biennial report written by Vee Burke.

The latest report, published in 2000, shows the cost of welfare rising to some $390 billion!

(You may be able to get a free copy by writing to the CRS, James Madison Building, 101 Independence Avenue SE, Washington, DC 20540.)

The number of welfare programs—actually eighty-one—is staggering, as is the fact that they are handled independently by six different cabinet agencies without a central, connecting computer. *Nobody*, not even the president, could find out how many programs any given welfare recipient is on—whether one or fifty—all designed to feed, clothe, house, educate, and heal America's poor.

They include well-known programs such as Medicaid, SSI, Earned Income Tax Credit, and food stamps. But there are a host of quite esoteric ones as well. For example:

- CAMP (College Assistance Migrant Program)
- Farm labor housing program
- Follow Through
- Foster grandparents
- Home investment partnerships
- Legal services
- Rural housing preservation grants
- Section 236 interest reduction payments
- Section 101 rent supplements
- Social service for Cuban/Haitian entrants
- State legalization impact assistance grants
- Summer food service for children
- Weatherization assistance
- What have you . . .

As the "welfare" (mostly unmarried women with children) rolls drop to a new all-time low, the total cost of the eighty-one welfare programs keeps rising. The last Congressional Research Service figure—$390 billion through 1998—is topped by a Heritage Foundation estimate of $407 billion. Of that, $296 billion is federal—leaving the Defense Department back in the fiscal dust.

The costs of welfare started out small, with a limited number of programs—until 1965, when they started their upward trend. Between 1965 and now, welfare cost the taxpayers over $7 trillion in current dollars. Yet almost as many people are below the poverty level as thirty-five years ago. (12 percent today versus 14 percent in 1965.)

On average, welfare adds almost $5,000 a year to the bill of each taxpaying family!

Some 1 percent.

But, you must be thinking, you're forgetting "welfare reform," the much-promoted propaganda effort of Uncle Sam.

No, I'm not forgetting that. In fact, that "reform" has raised the cost of welfare.

In 1994, AFDC, the much-publicized cash program for unwed mothers, cost us a total of $25.9 billion at the peak of the program when there were fourteen million people on it. The advent of prosperity cut into that bloated roster. In addition, in 1996 a welfare reform act was passed by Congress that forced the states to try to get people off the rolls and into work. By 1999, the number of people on the rolls had dropped to fewer than nine million, a cut of almost 40 percent.

The name of the program has been changed from AFDC to TANF, Temporary Assistance for Needy Families. The money for the states, who administer it, was also changed from a federal/state share to an outright block grant.

So with "reform" and such a massive cut in beneficiaries, we've saved billions of dollars—right?

Wrong. The last numbers available from the Health and Human Services Department, which runs TANF, shows a cost of $27.7 billion—a *rise of almost $2 billion*.

How is that possible? Easy. There are fewer people on welfare, but the costs of each family have risen. To help former welfare recipients adjust, the government has added an extra $2 billion a year for child care, plus still more money for transportation and job training, or, as the government jargon goes, "postemployment" services.

Welfare reform means fewer people on welfare, but more money out of the Treasury. Only in Washington.

So what should we do without disrupting the safety net?

That's easy. We just employ a little arithmetic and *really* eliminate poverty.

According to the Census Bureau, there are 7.7 million poor families (two or more people) in America, and 8.5 million poor individuals, for a total of 36.5 million poor people.

What if we decided to eliminate poverty with one swipe of the pen, and save a fortune in the process? Is it possible?

Watch me.

1. The first step is to eliminate *all* eighty-one welfare programs, closing down the scattershot operation in the six different cabinet agencies.

2. Set up a new agency called Department of Welfare, which does nothing else, has a central computer, and keeps real books.

3. We decide that there will be no more poverty in America. For an individual that level is defined as less than $8,178 income. For a family of two it is $10,468. For a family of three it is $12,803. For a family of four—the most common unit—it is $16,404, and upward with still more children.

4. Let's assume that the present average income of poor families is only $5,000 (probably an understatement) and that poor individuals have an average income of $4,000. We're going to get them all out of poverty. For the family of two, we're going to raise them to an $11,000 level. For a family of three, to a $13,000 level, and a family of four to $17,000, up to $25,000 for a family of seven. All done with a simple check.

For individuals, we're going to raise their income to $9,000, well above the poverty level.

How much will it cost to eliminate all poverty?

Simple. The average family of the 7.7 million poor will

need some $10,000 each annually to get out of poverty. The individuals will need some $5,000 to leave the roster of the disadvantaged.

The total outlay for the 8.5 million poor individuals will be $51 billion. For the 7.7 million poor families of from two to nine people, the cost will run around $80 billion a year.

5. **In addition, we give everyone an HMO subscription instead of Medicaid. According to the Mercer/Foster Higgins survey, that costs an employer $3,165 per employee, or about $1,500 per person. Now, not only will all poor people have an income above the poverty level, but they will all have health insurance.**

What will that Nirvana cost? Will it bankrupt the Treasury Building at Fourteenth and Pennsylvania? Hardly. Please continue to watch my moving pencil.

The check for families and individuals will cost $131 billion a year. The HMO for all 36.5 million poor people comes to $55 billion. We add another $25 billion for nursing homes, a real obligation of a concerned citizenry. We'll even add another $40 billion for odds and ends such as scholarships, student loans, and housing for the working poor above the poverty level.

We have now spent $251 billion and we've eliminated poverty, once and for all.

And in that grand process, we've saved $150 billion a year from the present $400 billion-plus welfare expenditure.

What do we do with the money now that we've gotten rid of almost all duplicating and ineffective eighty-one welfare programs, which have only succeeded in keeping people hopeful, surviving, but poor?

We put it in the bank to save it for a recession rainy day or start to truly pay down the national debt (see Chapter 3, Budget, for that scam).

Is there a flaw in the theory?

Sure. What are all those poverty-industry people, and social workers, and politicians, going to do for a living when everyone has enough?

Y

35

Youth At Risk

Have I Got a Teen Program for You!

As soon as someone says that the youth of America are "at risk," for whatever reason, the wheels of American government grind into motion.

Presidents make speeches, academics write tomes, psychologists psychologize, and most important, legislators legislate.

All that members of Congress need to get their names on a bill is a good cause, one that can be played to the naive voters, over and over again. Anyone familiar with how Washington works knows that there is no better cause than "teenagers at risk," whether for delinquency, substance abuse, alcoholism, suicide, or God knows what.

As a result, over the last thirty-five years, going back to the Eighty-ninth Congress of 1965, those occupying the benches of the House and historic desks of the Senate have been busy passing legislation—duplicating and overlapping themselves in order to "solve," once and for all, the "teenage dilemma," that elusive and often destructive behavior of adolescents that has bedeviled society for millennia.

As the General Accounting Office says:

"Multiple federal departments and agencies spend billions of dollars funding a wide variety of programs serving at-risk and delinquent youth. Many of the programs are potentially duplicative, providing services that appear to overlap those of other federal programs in the same agency or in other agencies, and many provide multiple services." This, they fear, results in "inefficient services."

Cutting across the governmentese, how "multiple" and how "duplicative"? How many youth programs are we actually talking about?

Are there as many as ten teenage programs? Could they be stretched out in as many as four government agencies?

Try not to smile. According to the GAO, teens are the most massively overwatched and overtreated people in the land of the Beltway.

There are 127 teenage programs being handled by fifteen different federal agencies, a glut of duplication and ignorance that rivals all other overlaps in a government that thrives on that special variety of waste.

But how much could it cost? As much as $100 million a year?

Loosen your fiscal imagination. The cost of teen programs runs more than $4 billion a year, a massive waste of money.

This happens because in our system, as soon as a congressman passes a "teen bill," no matter how many similar ones have been passed before, a separate bureaucracy is set up by the executive branch, willy-nilly.

Many of the same programs for teens are located in different agencies, who try to do the very same job. For instance, twenty teen programs designed to treat substance abuse are located in thirteen different federal agencies, each with its own staff and budget.

Several programs are also located in the same agency doing the same job. Within the Justice Department there are nine separate programs trying to do the same job of providing substance abuse prevention.

The 127 programs come out of not only expected agencies, but peculiar ones as well. In addition to HHS and Education, even HUD and Justice, which you might expect, there are programs for delinquent teens and teens at risk in *Agriculture, Labor, Treasury, Interior, Transportation, and even the National Endowment for the Arts.*

(When Washington feels that there is fertile ground to "help," no matter what the cost or how weak the theory, they truly let themselves go.)

The program definitions are as varied as they are duplicated. They include "capital improvement" (whatever that means); research and evaluation; self-sufficiency skills; parental intervention; violence intervention; monitoring; substance abuse prevention and treatment; tutoring; and, of course, counseling.

Does this champion work in duplication, overlap, and inflated cost do any good?

Apparently no one knows. And probably not.

Legislators pass the bills to gain headlines and to feel good about themselves and politics. No one reports back before it becomes law that the bill is not needed—that there are already 126 similar bureaucracies doing much the same thing. The President signs the new and popular "teenage bill," and the executive branch works hard to hire experts and other bureaucrats, then spends what Congress appropriates, whether it is foolish or not.

Still, no one knows if it does any good, and most suspect it is a monumental failure.

As the GAO says in one of its reports:

"From a decision making standpoint, what is needed—but is often not available—is information about the overall effectiveness of a particular program. That is, to what extent are individual programs, such as the Safe and Drug Free Schools and Communities Act of 1994 program, achieving the expected results?"

Of course, those familiar with government programs will be skeptical about any reported "results."

What should we do?

First, combine all 127 programs into 4:

1. **Drug abuse**
2. **Alcohol abuse**
3. **Violence**
4. **Job training**

Put the first two in National Institutes of Health. Put the third in Justice, and the fourth in Labor. Close down the other 123 programs in the fifteen agencies, and save some $3.5 billion a year.

Adolescence is often a time of hormonal madness, which can be exacerbated by cultural peer pressure. That will always be with us, but it is more severe today because of the overly permissive, standardless *adult* society, which provides a poor model for youth.

Teenagers have been mystifying adults since Romeo and Juliet, and before. Don't expect Washington to change that, especially with *only* 127 programs.

Z

36

***

Zooming National Debt
It Still Goes Only One Way—Up

Washington frantically, and falsely, boasts that with the supposed surplus, which is almost entirely "borrowed" Social Security (FICA) taxes, the national debt is being paid off.

This is merely another Beltway delusion that has reached such a fantasy level that it must be challenged, and countered. The reality is that the national debt, as recorded honestly by only one source—the Bureau of the Public Debt of the Treasury Department—is rising steadily and inexorably, minute by minute, as we speak. In most years, it goes up some $100 billion a year, some $2 billion a week, and some $300 million a day.

So what's behind this latest piece of Beltway propaganda meant to divert taxpayers from the fact that some 25 percent of their FICA taxes are being stolen? Obviously, once again our politicians are cooking the books.

As we've seen, the national debt comes in two parts, enabling politicians to play one against the other. The so-called "public" debt is actually quite nonpublic, being held heavily by financial institutions. That is the marketable portion of the debt, the "external" part.

The other portion is the "internal" debt, the true "public" one, which is held by the government from monies paid in from our FICA taxes for Social Security. Those trillions have been paid in *by us* to Social Security, then squandered in the general fund, violating the public's trust. We paid our excess Social Security taxes under the assumption—which turned out to be false—that it was all going to care for the aged, widows, orphans, and the disabled.

The total of the two debts, called the national debt, as of the end of fiscal 1996 (September 30), was $5.22 trillion. By the end of 1997, it had zoomed to $5.41 trillion. At the conclusion of fiscal 1998—the year of the heralded first "surplus"—it magically went up again, rising to $5.53 trillion, a jump of $113 billion. At the end of 1999, a period of supposed enormous surplus, the national debt rose another $130 billion. At the end of fiscal 2000 on September 30, 2000, says the Bureau of Public Debt (Department of Treasury), it was once again *higher* than the previous year, reaching $5,674,178,000,000.

The debt seems to defy the laws of arithmetic gravity. As the surplus gets larger and the debt is supposedly being "paid down," instead it continues to rise.

And what of the future? The president's own 2001 budget has a revealing chart that shows the national debt rising each year, until it reaches $6.8 trillion by 2013, the year the boomers come heavily on line for Social Security!

So if the debt is going up, are we really paying off the debt?

Hardly. It's all part of a Beltway trick. That's easily revealed by the monthly statement from the Bureau of the Public Debt which has year-over-year comparisons of *both* parts of the debt, external and internal. The latter represents your FICA tax surpluses that have been all spent and exchanged for IOUs. To convert those government promissory notes into checks for the aged, and to replace what has been spent in a frenzy of profligacy and waste, will require enormous tax increases or reduced benefits. Both plans are now being organized by Washington, but not talked about.

Now over the $1 trillion level, those Social Security IOUs will rise to $4 trillion by 2013, money down the drain to the tune of $100,000 per present aged retiree. Instead of spending that money in the general treasury, as they have done, they could have sent that windfall to the aged, or reduced the FICA taxes for everyone by some 20 percent. But no: that would require a concerned, intelligent federal government—a missing ingredient in the equation.

The scam of cooked books has now reached fruition. Naturally, the overall national debt went *up*, not *down*.

Perhaps equally important, the interest that we have to pay on the total debt went up, as we have seen, not down, as Washington claims. So we pay four times:

1. Our FICA taxes are much higher than they should be.

2. The Social Security surplus of some $175 billion in 2000 was taken by the general fund and spent—on everything from Welfare, defense, 127 youth programs, to 194 federal golf courses.

3. The government gives Social Security an IOU for the misspent money. It is intrinsically worthless and has to be redeemed by $4 trillion in cash in 2013, with no idea where we can get the money.

4. Not only have we lost $4 trillion, but that increases our interest bill by $240 billion a year, more than we save by paying down part of the "external" debt.

Can anything be done to reduce, not increase, the zooming national debt? Yes.

1. First, we should pass the Moynihan-Kerrey bill to return Social Security to pay-as-you-go, as it was before 1983. This will reduce our FICA taxes immediately.

2. Second, without an excess FICA tax, there will be no Social Security surplus to spend, thereby reducing the "internal" debt.

3. With a smaller internal debt, the amount we pay in interest will drop enormously.

4. The savings in interest will enable us to truly pay off the internal debt year by year, using that money plus any *real* surplus. Instead of cooked books, the government accounting will start to be honest.

Most important, new legislation is required to split the so-called unified budget, which permits the current shenanigans, into two: the general fund and the Social Security fund. *That legislation will make it illegal to borrow any funds from Social Security and will start to pay down the $1 trillion now owed to the Social Security fund.*

Is that impossible? Not if we can get our politicians in both parties to become educated about fiscal affairs by going to accounting school, then start to tell the truth and drop the obfuscation about the "surplus," the Social Security fund, and the ever-growing national debt.

Anyone for $7 trillion?

PART TWO

REVIEW AND DÉJÀ VU

Defeats and Victories
in the Fight Against Waste

Each time I appeared before a congressional committee, or spoke on radio and television, the hope was that the words were not wasted—that through my efforts and those of my allies in the fight for better government (and there are many), Washington would take heed.

In some cases they have, but in most they have continued on their cavalier way even though the American public wants smaller, better government. Sometimes citizens are less than vocal as they *temporarily* resign themselves to the inevitable Washington callousness.

In this section I will review several suggestions made in my original volume of 1992, and show which have made a dent and which have been treated with indifference. Even though many dedicated members of Congress have worked, often futilely, to cut the pork, fat, and ludicrous spending in both unnecessary and failed federal programs, the debacle of waste continues.

Follow me through this catalog of frustration and *occasional* victory.

OFFICE OF FORMER SPEAKERS

Back in 1992, in a quarterly report of disbursements of the House of Representatives, I spotted an interesting appropriation, for the Office of Former Speakers. I had never heard of it, and neither had the talented Capitol phone operators who had been with the Congress for twenty-five years or, for that matter, the Speaker's Office itself.

I researched the secret and found that each former Speaker of the House received a magnificent *lifetime* perk, which included a nice office and three staff members in his hometown after retirement. The top staffer could have a salary of $96,000, which back in hometown America is an exceptionally healthy remuneration.

So what did the former Speakers do in their new digs? Absolutely nothing except greet a few guests and take advantage of the unknowing generosity of the beleaguered taxpayers—to the collective tune of $700,000 a year.

When I wrote about it in 1992, it struck the imagination (and shame) of some members of Congress, who in 1993 amended the old law and cut the former Speakers' freebie to a five-year term.

Thomas "Tip" O'Neill, who had his "former" office in Boston, has since passed away, and the last former Speaker, Tom Foley of Washington State, has gone on to become ambassador to Japan. The remaining two formers, Jim Wright of Fort Worth, Texas, and Carl Albert of Oklahoma City, have closed their offices on September 30, 1998, as their free time ran out.

But wait, a staff of three and an office back in Georgia is now using taxpayer money for the now-retired Speaker Newt

Gingrich. I hate to play spoilsport with an i/
but Congress should take that last, definiti
program down entirely. It just wastes $27
mer Speaker.

Modifying the program from lifetime to five years was a
small, if symbolic, victory for the American taxpayer over the
Washington behemoth. Now we have to go all the way, with a
nod of apology to Mr. Gingrich and new Speaker Dennis
Hastert (R., IL), who'll just have to fend for themselves with
only six-figure retirement checks.

Just close down the meaningless Office of Former Speakers.

GOVERNMENT AIRPLANES, NONMILITARY

I discovered (by accident) that the U.S. government owns and
operates a giant fleet of twelve hundred civilian planes, with
pilots, airfields, mechanics, and all that's needed to keep them
flying. Worse yet, the planes are from twenty-five different manufacturers, with different spare parts and complex maintenance.

The purpose? Ostensibly for official government business;
but there has been evidence that top bureaucrats from many
agencies around the country have used the planes so they don't
have to mix with sweaty taxpayers like us in airports, with no
evidence the abuse has been stopped. The cost? Some $2 billion
for the planes, $200 million a year for depreciation, and $800
million a year for upkeep. Worse yet, there's the cost of the use
of airports, both civilian and military. *And* the government
leases still more planes at the added cost of $100 million annu-
ally.

A check of two planes owned by the Department of Transportation (DOT) showed that several of the flights ordered by
top bureaucrats and Coast Guard brass included spouses and
guests, casting grave doubt on the *official* use of the aircraft.

People in government thought I had temporarily lost it because the concept of twelve hundred civilian planes seemed like a reporter's fantasy. Fortunately, former senator James R. Sasser of Tennessee, now ambassador to China, asked the inspector general of the DOT to check out our civilian fleet. It not only confirmed my figures, but showed even more serious waste.

In fact, I was wrong on the number. *There aren't 1,200 planes, but 1,384.* The confusion comes from the fact that 152 are missing—most scooped up illegally by state and local governments. By checking FAA records, the IG also learned that thirty-one of the planes were registered to four government agencies that weren't supposed to have any aircraft.

There were other findings of government madness. It turns out the U.S. Forest Service *gave away* thirty-five of the planes to private contractors, a move that the General Services Administration, which oversees the $65 million boondoggle, called illegal. Worse yet, one of the contractors had the chutzpah, unmitigated gall, to lease the government's own planes back to them for Desert Storm, collecting $920,000 in the deal. One man who arranged most of the plane swaps made more than $1 million reselling four of the aircraft.

Do we need this giant fleet of almost fourteen hundred planes? Of course not. Former secretary of transportation Federico Peña was surprised that his department had 304 planes, but even more alarmed to learn that the two assigned to him—including one that cost $24 million—were sitting mainly *unused* on the tarmac at National Airport in Washington. (He says he flew coach.)

The answer, of course, is not another IG report, but a swift kick in the consciousness of the House Subcommittee on Transportation and Infrastructure, which handles the General Services Administration, to get them to sell two-thirds of the planes. That will allow the high-flying bureaucrats the thrill of sitting next to thee and me on ordinary commercial flights.

This is a major déjà vu *defeat* for the taxpayers.

DECORATING FOR THE BUREAUCRACY

Government employees, especially those in the higher echelons, *love* to spend taxpayer money on expensive furnishings. For example, the Clintons redid the Oval Office, which was quite beautiful before, for an estimated $400,000 to suit their taste.

That, of course, is petty cash compared with the estimated $1.3 billion that I posited in 1992 as the annual cost of decorating and redecorating federal offices. When I called the OMB, which has since become a semimute organization, and asked about this cost, I was told there was "no such item as decorating in the federal budget."

They said I would have to call each agency, but added that they believed it would be futile: no one would tell me their allotment. It seems that decorating, like the congressional recording studios, is a "black hole" when it comes to public information. What we don't know, they figure, won't aggravate us.

I pressed on into the world of know-nothing and found a lead. One official of the National Furniture Center in suburban Virginia told me that GSA did not buy furniture, but is contracted with manufacturers for discounts, which many agencies used. He did a computer run for me and learned that in a recent fiscal year they had handled $676 million to buy everything from desks to rugs to pictures.

He estimated that since some departments, like Defense, did their own buying, that number represented a third to a half the decorating total—which would then be $1.3–$2 billion, a figure I published in the original *Government Racket*.

When *20/20*, the television program, decided to do a piece on me and my book, they approached GSA, which screamed that my figure was outlandishly high—hinting that I was a liar. They could "account for" only $515 million in decorating that year. "Account for" turned out to be the verbal gimmick to relieve them of real accountability.

I called my lead, Mr. Mike Bielski, who confirmed the $676 million as only part of the total. At GSA's request, *20/20* attended a meeting with them to go over the numbers.

"We had our meeting," the *20/20* producer recounts. "I told them what you had learned. Suddenly it was no longer only $515 that they had spent. In the last moments they had found another $250 million-plus, and their total was now $765 [million]. But, they admitted, it was no longer all the government decorating bill. They figured that maybe it was eighty percent. So now they were suddenly admitting that the annual decorating bill was about a billion. It had almost doubled in a half-hour meeting."

One customer, the head of Federal Program Management, a private company that helps furniture manufacturers get federal contracts, thinks that both I and the GSA are underestimating the real bill—which he puts at $3 billion a year.

When the *20/20* producer was at the Department of the Interior, he admired the nice new furniture. "Oh," said a government spokesman, "we didn't want it. We had perfectly good furniture, but the government people *insisted* that we buy new stuff."

What happened to Mike Bielski, you might ask? He was immediately lifted out of his vital job in furniture and given some credit-card responsibility in bureaucratic Siberia. Mike was a casualty in the war against bad government, and should be honored—not castigated—by the executive branch, where the buck stops in the White House.

Now the wasteful decorating program goes on as before, with the General Services Administration saying they have no comment on the size of expenditures.

This is a sorry case of déjà vu, and a continuing defeat for the taxpayer.

HELIUM

Probably because it resembles hot air in its lifting power, the revelation that the government was spending a small fortune producing helium received an enormous amount of publicity. I appeared on more than one television show discussing it, and one TV magazine show actually went to Amarillo, Texas, to show the National Helium Reserve boondoggle in operation.

The government's helium expenditure was ridiculous—about $25 million in above-market helium purchases from the federally owned plant, plus salary and benefits for 215 workers, plus the interest on a debt of $1.4 billion, for a total of some $125 million a year.

How did it all begin? Washington went into the helium business when they needed the nonflammable gas for military blimps in 1925, a need that soon disappeared. Now, some of it is useful in the space program, but it could be bought from private producers—who extract it from natural gas—much more cheaply.

The public cried foul about the government manufacturing helium, or anything else. That cry became a wail when people learned that Washington had a billion dollars' worth of the gas, enough to last one hundred years, stored underground in Texas.

Vice President Gore jumped in, suggesting that we "improve" the situation by cutting the program 10 percent as an example of his propagandistic "reinventing" government program.

Pressure rose to close down the needless operation, but pork advocates protected it for four years, until finally, in 1996, H.R. 4168, the "Helium Privatization Act"—designed to sell off the assets to private industry—passed 411–10 in the House, then went through the Senate and became law.

This was a reasonably important victory for the American taxpayer. We retrieved a good piece of change and we got Uncle Sam out of one of his last flings as a bumbling manufacturer.

CONGRESSIONAL LSOs

In the world of congressional perks, nothing was as outrageous as the Legislative Service Organizations, an opportunity for members of the House to enjoy themselves in luncheons, parties, and meetings for their favorite interest—all at taxpayer expense. In my 1992 volume I exposed this political near-fraud, and asked that they be closed posthaste.

The LSO "clubs" were as close to legal skulduggery as you can get. Organized as the "caucuses" based on geography, ethnic background, or interests—from the Hispanic Caucus to the Pennsylvania group to the Space Caucus—they spent some $5 million a year indulging themselves. Dues for these exclusive clubs ran as high as $10,000 a year, all paid by the taxpayers from the congressmen's expense accounts.

There were twenty-eight of these operations, with a combined staff of eighty-eight federal employees. They proved to be quite generous with our money. The Pennsylvania state caucus spent $7,699 for a single-cocktail party, and the New York delegation honored a retiring member with a $1,466 Steuben glass eagle.

They were also sloppy, to say the least, with taxpayer money. A courageous audit of their books by the office of Congressman Pat Roberts of Kansas turned out startling information. "We found that up to $7.7 million is just plain missing and could not be accounted for," said a spokesman for Roberts.

Finally, when the truth came to light, the LSOs could not stand the illumination. In 1995, as part of the legislative appropriations bill, they were closed.

Problem is that the $7.7 million is still missing.

This was a nice small victory for still-suffering taxpayers.

MINING LAW OF 1872

In the wide, wide universe of federal cons, nothing stands out like the abuse of the Mining Law of 1872, a piece of legislation now over 125 years old, whose time for extinction has really come.

Under that archaic law, as exposed by me and others in 1992 and in considerable publicity since, the government sold "hard-rock" mineral land for $2.50 to $5.00 an acre, the original price set in 1872. Never mind that $5 should now be well over $1,000 after inflation, the practice still continues.

Since 1872, the government has, under the "patent" provision of the law, sold off a piece of land the size of the entire state of Connecticut. A House committee states that in just the last thirty years we have given away some $100 *billion* in minerals—gold, silver, copper, and platinum—for a pittance.

In one tragic but quite typical case, a citizen bought ("patented") seventeen thousand acres of public land from the Department of the Interior for $42,500. A few weeks later, he turned around and sold it to an oil company. What did he receive? Even you couldn't guess: $37 million, cash that should have gone into the Treasury to alleviate the pain of taxpayers.

This boondoggle has few peers in Washington's misguided history of waste. Some $2.50-an-acre parcels near a growing gambling-casino town in Nevada are appraised at $200,000 an acre.

Even the federal government, as slow as its consciousness operates, is beginning to understand that this is massive legal fraud. Secretary of Interior Bruce Babbitt calls the 1872 law "a legal rip-off of public resources." He points out that it made sense in General Grant's administration when the West was still wide open and the law helped to develop the country. The prospector paid the low price, no royalties, and had to invest $100 a year, which at the time was real money, in the land.

Today that sum is ludicrous. Since 1993, mining interests have paid a meager $25,000 for resources valued at *$15 billion!* And they still pay zero royalties when they take the gold, for example, out of the ground. On April 28, 1998, sixty-two acres on Prince of Wales Island in Alaska was bought from the government for only $155 even though it contains an estimated $80 million in 2.3 million tons of iron, with recoverable copper, gold, and silver.

Some of the galling rip-offs include:

American Barrick (owned by a Canadian company) went to court and forced Interior to cede nineteen hundred acres of gold-saturated land in Nevada for some $10,000. Their Goldstrike Mine is estimated to hold 22.5 million ounces of gold worth $10 billion.

In addition to the multibillion-dollar rip-offs, there are small ones that are no less galling. A nineteen-acre granite operation near Phoenix was sold by the government in 1987 for $47, and is now valued at $3.8 million.

Though the federal lands are ostensibly bought for mining rights, they can be sold by the new owners simply as good real estate, especially as part of a ski complex. In Keystone, Colorado, for instance, a 160-acre parcel was patented for $400. No gold had been mined, but a portion of the parcel is close to the Keystone ski runs and was up for sale as part of a real estate development deal. The asking price of the $2.50 land was $11,000 per acre.

Is all land bought from Uncle Sam royalty-proof? Apparently not. Only "hard-rock claims" get away with this witless legal racket. By contrast, those who actually "mine" coal, iron, and gas from public lands pay a royalty to Uncle Sam of up to 12 percent.

Congress, led by House and Senate members in the West, apparently likes giving away our gold and silver to the newest robber barons. Others in Congress have been fighting them, especially now-retired Senator Dale Bumpers of Arkansas, who sponsored S. 326 and S. 327, the latter of which would fix the price of the patent at the *fair market value* of the land and its minerals. It would also add a royalty on the minerals taken out. Hearings were held, but so far it has not even gotten out of the Subcommittee on Forests and Public Land Management, which controls the mad Mining Law of 1872.

One last disturbing thought. *The majority of gold mines ripped off from the taxpayers under this law are controlled by foreign investments—making much of the West a colonial outpost of other nations.*

What should we do?

Naturally, close this iniquitous period in our history. Those senators and House members who continue to support ludicrous government regulations such as selling our land for $2.50 an acre should be ousted, posthaste, by the voters.

This is a continuing major defeat for the taxpayers.

WOOL AND MOHAIR

When I first wrote about this, I subtitled it "Shearing the Public," an apt description of a Department of Agriculture and Department of Defense coalition that has needlessly cost us a fortune.

In 1954 Defense was worried that American sheep farmers might not produce enough wool for warm uniforms and coats for the armed forces. They declared wool a "strategic" commodity and asked Agriculture to help sheep farmers increase their production.

Congress quickly passed the National Wool Act, which set up an enormous subsidy for farmers, which since then has cost the taxpayers $2 billion!

The humorous, or tragic, aspect of the program is that by 1960, just six years later, the Pentagon told Agriculture it no longer needed help. It was using only 8 percent of domestic wool production, and synthetic fabrics were replacing wool in cold-weather clothing for Alaska and other frigid areas.

The Pentagon was out of it, but the sheep lobby had its horns (to mix a metaphor) into the Treasury. By the time I had written about this farce in 1992, it had been going on for thirty-eight years, and was draining the taxpayer to the tune of $100 million a year. Meanwhile, another commodity, mohair—the hair of Angora goats—had sneaked into the program without the blessings of the Pentagon.

After the exposure of this expensive program in my book, and subsequently on television, a shamed Congress moved into action.

On July 27, 1993, the Senate passed the Department of Agriculture and Rural Development Appropriations Act. Senator Richard Bryan (D., NV) included an amendment to cut off the wool and mohair subsidies, which had then reached a $190 million-a-year level. Just before the vote on the full appropriation, a motion was offered to return the entire bill to committee to eliminate the Bryan amendment. The Senate voted sixty-three to thirty-six to kill the motion to recommit. The Bryan amendment won and the wool and mohair scam became a thing of the past—even as it left the Treasury $2 billion poorer.

A nice victory for America, for which I take some credit.

RURAL UTILITIES SERVICES

The REA, the Rural Electrification Administration, was one of the great successes of the New Deal. In the 1930s and 1940s, the wonders of electricity had not reached most American farms, only 10 percent of which had power.

The government loaned money to small electric cooperatives at 2 percent, then the going rate. By 1952, 90 percent of rural America was electrified. By 1960, the figure had reached 98 percent.

But instead of declaring victory and closing shop, the program has been expanded over the last forty years and has become, in the tradition of the modern American government, one of the prime examples of corporate welfare—using our tax money to make businesses richer while we get poorer.

The operation is mainly a bank: they loan money to set up small electrical companies. But instead of cutting back on loans once the nation was electrified, they started loaning out more money than ever before. At last count, they had a loan portfolio of *$37.5 billion outstanding* to over seventeen hundred cooperatives, making it one of Washington's many big banks—albeit one of the most inefficient ones.

In just the few years between fiscal 1994 and June 30, 1997, the RUS made over $3 billion more in loans to old electrical cooperatives.

Is the money safe? No one really knows, but recent signs are not good. *Just a few years ago, the agency had to write off $1.7 billion in electricity loans as a total loss.* Worse yet, more write-offs—money you and I will have to swallow—are anticipated.

According to a government audit, some $8 billion of the principal is being held by "borrowers experiencing financial problems," a way of preparing us for the reality that there will be still more money down the drain.

One of the tragicomic aspects of the RUS is that a number of government-subsidized small utilities provide really cheap power to such unneedy towns as Vail and Las Vegas, lighting them up for the rich on the average taxpayer's nickel.

One particularly wasteful activity was loaning out money for years at 5 percent interest when the government had to buy the money for 7, even 10, percent, making each loan a loser from the beginning. Only recently have most cooperatives been paying a bit above the Treasury's cost of money.

Unfortunately, once a federal agency is set up, it looks for other areas in which to spend money. The REA, now known as the Rural Utilities Services, decided to expand into rural telephone service, which has become a large government-business partnership. They started hundreds of small telephone cooperatives, many of which became more successful than their electricity cousins. Soon giants like GTE and Alltell started to buy them up, taking the sweetheart 5 percent government loans at a time when money cost 8 to 10 percent. So in addition to helping smaller co-ops, we were subsidizing giant corporations with taxpayer money.

But even though the telephone operations are making money, the government continues to play banker with your cash. In the same two-year period, these telephone operations got $1.8 billion in new money from RUS.

Nothing has improved since 1992, when I first wrote about the REA. If anything, things have gotten worse with that large

$1.7 billion loss. The answer, of course, is to stop all new loans and set up a closeout operation to collect as much as we can of the $37 billion outstanding, then eliminate the Rural Utilities Service.

Congress doesn't seem to be listening. *In this case, the taxpayer has taken a severe shellacking.*

ESSENTIAL AIR

This is a most peculiar program, one Americans know little about.

A doctor and his wife got on a plane in Boston to go to Bar Harbor, Maine, a swanky resort town where they luxuriated for the month of September. They flew Colgan Airways in a propellor plane and spent only $150 for a roundtrip ticket, an amazingly low price. They were happy with the service and asked little else. In fact, what is there to ask?

Meanwhile, an affluent advertising executive in Boston prepared to go skiing at Killington in Vermont. He bought a ticket for a Colgan Airways flight to Rutland, Vermont, at that same super discount fare of $150 round trip. There he rented a car and drove twenty minutes to Killington and Pico slopes, skis and all.

So what's so peculiar about these flights?

Just one thing. The vacationers paid particularly low fares because Uncle Sam was paying the lion's share of it in a stroke of generosity that we don't—and shouldn't—appreciate.

Is it just an occasional flight on Colgan where you get a government-discounted ticket? Hardly. The plane between Boston and the lovely coast of Maine leaves four times a day so you don't have to miss a minute of vacation. And the route to the ski slopes is also flown four times daily on weekdays.

The program is called Essential Air, a hyped name chosen by the government mainly because the travel is blatantly "*non-*

essential." It's not just an East Coast recreation goodie, but a national operation that lets you fly out of one hundred cities at a low, low fare subsidized by the government.

The rationale? Not every city in America has scheduled airline service, so if you are more than forty-five miles away from a scheduled airline, *the federal government will pay an airline to come in to fly you away!*

Such service might make sense in Alaska, with its small population and big distances, but in almost all of the rest of the country, it's a mere boondoggle, a fancy piece of pork arranged by congressmen in collusion with the Department of Transportation.

The numbers are startling. Back in 1992, when I first exposed this nonsense, there were 130 destinations getting federal aid at a total cost of $38 million a year. By 1999 there were only 103 destinations, but the cost had risen to $51 million.

Where does the money come from? Originally from the general fund. But now, every time you buy a plane ticket, 10 percent goes into the Airport Trust Fund, which then sends a check to their favorite subsidized airline.

So who gets the money and who doesn't? The eligibility is based on whether the government fears that you might tire by having to drive too far to get to your nearest airport. So if your town is more than forty-five miles from a scheduled airline hub, you might be in line for air-ticket welfare. In most states it makes little sense, because distances to hubs are not that great. Even in Big Sky, Montana, which gets over $2 million to fly folks into Billings, there is no speed limit in the daytime—and if you lust for the lack of crowds, there's no reason someone in Chicago should pay for it.

The subsidies are overgenerous, with several airlines getting over $1 million for each route. As a general rule, Uncle Sam picks up three fourths of the ticket price, and the passenger, rich, poor, or otherwise, pays only one fourth.

When I exposed Essential Air, the media, especially TV, highlighted the scam of a subsidized airline flying Washington VIPs to Hot Springs, Virginia, to stay at the prestigious Homestead, and vacationers to Hyannis Port so they could luxuriate on the public's nickel.

So what's happened since?

The government cut out Hot Springs and Hyannis Port because of bad publicity. Chastised for a while, they actually cut back the taxpayer tab from $38 million to $22 million by 1996. But when things cooled, the politicians pushed it back to over $50 million.

This program should be closed in its entirety and the airline ticket tax eliminated. People locate where they want, and you and I shouldn't have to pay for it.

This is a defeat for the average citizen—unless he wants to ski in Vermont or go fishing in Bar Harbor.

FEDERAL EMPLOYEES

Some of the major costs in the bloated federal government are the bloated payroll, bloated benefits, and bloated retirement, along with the bloated overhead. Altogether we're talking about more than a third of a *trillion* dollars a year, a sizable portion of which is wasted.

Back in 1992, and again in 1994, there was much talk about reducing the number of federal employees. Extravagant promises were made by the President and the Congress, which pledged to reduce their own staffs by 25 percent.

How has that worked out?

The Congress, which had thirty-eight thousand employees in

January 1993, has reduced that number by seventy-five hundred, or a 20 percent cut, for which they should receive a smidgen of praise. But of course that branch had a bare six thousand employees in 1950, only one fifth its present size.

The comparison is best demonstrated by the fact that in Harry Truman's time, each member of the House had only five employees. Today that number is eighteen full-time plus four part-time. In the Senate, the number of employees per member has grown fivefold. Today each senator has an average staff of forty people, not counting those in his committees—a ridiculous load for taxpayers.

Despite glowing promises, the White House has done nothing to reduce its staff. When FDR was president during the depression, he ran the nation with fewer than two hundred people in the White House. Harry Truman did fine with 285, and JFK with 375. By George Bush's time, the White House staff had escalated to over 1,100—without counting the Office of Management and Budget.

And today? According to a recent budget, there are now 1,200 employees in the White House, with absolutely no cut.

Since 1993, the promise to cut the number of federal employees has been *partially* carried out. In January 1993 there were 2,188,847 on the payroll, excluding post office employees. Today there are 1,869,452, a cut of 319,395.

One imagines the decimation of employees in one in seven offices throughout the vast government empire. But the numbers are deceiving. *Most of those cuts have come in one agency, the Department of Defense, which has been more than decimated in strength.* (We could still beat Guatemala in a close fight.) The cut in defense employment was 239,000, leaving only a 90,000 reduction throughout the rest of government, or some 4 percent. In fact, five agencies have had an *increase* in manpower.

Why is reduction of personnel so important? Because being a government employee today is not only a sinecure, but a well-paid one, a reversal of pre-World War II conditions. Federal employees earn more and get more benefits than the average American. The average federal salary is now $45,000, including the bottom of the list, which is some 40 percent higher than the paycheck of the typical American. Staffers such as administrative assistants (AAs) to Congressmen earn as much as $110,000 a year.

Benefits of federal employees are also extravagant—75 percent higher than those of the average worker, including up to five weeks vacation, plus sick leave. Retirement pay is among the nation's best. Overall, each federal employee costs us—in wages, benefits, and retirement—some $85,000 a year.

Yes, we've had a small gain for the taxpayers, but mainly in the badly decimated Defense Department, which is more strategically important than most government agencies.

But it's not nearly enough in the other agencies, a fertile field for cutting personnel, drastically. The payroll is still badly inflated.

The answer is to eliminate another half million employees, or some 25 percent, within the next five years, and do it harmlessly. That's possible because attrition is high in federal employment. According to the Office of Personnel Management, over 7 percent of the government work force retires, dies, or leaves each year.

That means an automatic reduction of 130,000 personnel yearly if no one is replaced. Instead, we should replace only 30,000 and eliminate the rest of the jobs. The savings from those half million former workers would be $42 billion over a period of five years.

Not counted here is the overhead of the government—rent, telephone, and other costs, which are estimated at some $200 billion a year. *If* we could cut some of that overhead simultaneously with the loss of employees, we would save another $35 billion a year.

But won't we miss a half million workers? The answer from one who deals regularly with federal employees is a resounding "No." No one will miss the federal employees who leave by attrition. In fact, I venture that no one will know that they are gone.

The government will probably operate more efficiently. Today federal employees have every conceivable opportunity not to work. Through a gimmick called "flex time," they can put in ten-hour days from Monday to Thursday and take Friday off. Or they can come in to work at 6:00 A.M. and leave at 2:00 P.M., making them quite inefficient. That early in the morning there are few fellow employees to work with, and little contact is possible with the outside world. One federal employee told me she passes the flex time doing crossword puzzles.

The half million personnel cut, with accompanying overhead reduction, will save us an additional $50 billion a year, enough for a massive tax cut.

Once that happens, we can assess the scene again. My guess is that the federal civilian roster would still be bloated. We might be able to cut it another 25 percent, leaving it at one million, or half the present size, with probably still greater efficiency.

I, for one, am game to try.

Meanwhile, whatever happened to that 25 percent promised cut in the White House staff?

This is the *smallest* of victories for the taxpayer, with much more needed.

CONGRESSIONAL RETIREMENT

One of the great advantages of being a member of Congress is that you get to retire earlier (as young as fifty) and much more comfortably than either other government employees or most constituents, who are often limited to their Social Security checks.

Tom Foley of Washington State, former Speaker of the House, left Washington after being defeated locally at the polls. But he left with a $123,000-a-year pension, which means that some $3 million will be coming to him over the rest of his normal life expectancy.

Of those members who retired beginning in January 1997, one will receive $100,000 a year and ten more retirees will receive pensions larger than the $89,500 salary they had before the huge, controversial pay raise of 1991.

The National Taxpayers Union, a large antiwaste organization, has created an intriguing chart showing how much retirees from Congress will receive over the years. For those who are not federal employees, it is sinus-clearing. Former House member Pat Schroeder of Colorado, for instance, is only in her late fifties, so she has many years in which to receive her pension, which began at $74,915 in 1997. But since inflation increases that pension yearly, and the years go by, we can estimate that she will eventually take home $4,182,573.

How did their pensions get so extravagant? Most of the members who came in before 1984 put 8 percent of their salary into the retirement fund. Taxpayers added approximately *three dollars for every one of theirs,* making it possible for retired members to receive their hefty checks.

Besides, the size of their retirement check is figured from the three highest years of salary, so when members got their enormous pay raise in 1991, their pensions jumped up accordingly.

And worse (or better, depending on your position), members are protected from inflation and receive a yearly COLA, cost-of-living, increase, in their pension check—something 90 percent of private retirement plans do not provide. Within a decade or less after retirement, many members will have a pension check larger than their former salary.

We are building up an enormous unfunded liability in our congressional pension plan, money we will owe to increasingly longer-living "formers."

One peculiar twist of congressional retirement benefits came to light when Tom Schatz, president of Citizens Against Government Waste, called for an end to giving pensions to former members of Congress who are convicted felons. It seems that fourteen former members of Congress who are convicted criminals continue to receive mostly taxpayer-paid pensions totaling $667,000 a year. The CAGW has supported legislation to rescind these pensions.

The whole question of congressional retirement requires establishing a new, different plan. Probably the answer is to scrap the present retirement system. Instead members should receive Social Security when they come of age, plus a 401K plan in which the government will match their contribution.

In any case, it sometimes becomes clear why members of Congress fight so hard to get reelected, and succeed 93 percent of the time.

What Americans can only dream of is how to become a congressman—without having to raise a million dollars to run for office.

In this retirement battle, the taxpayers have not only lost, but the defeat lingers on year by year.

AUCTIONING OFF THE AIRWAVES

Speaking of cash, back in 1992 I stuck my neck out and suggested that *giving away* one of the nation's prized assets, the airwaves, was a foolish, wasteful system.

The tradition at the Federal Communications Commission was that since the airwaves were owned by the people, why not return it to them free of charge, by lottery? So for years they set up this gambling pool for which you paid $200 to enter. If they picked your number out of a hat—voilà, you now owned a megahertz band worth maybe a few million dollars, or perhaps even $10 *billion*.

When I wrote *The Government Racket*, it took little intelligence to realize that the FCC, like many government operations, was long on airwave bands, but short on the one commodity it needed most: brains.

"The way we did it made no sense. It lost billions for the government," says an FCC official, talking about one of the biggest giveaways in the history of the nation.

Those airwaves, technically referred to as the "radio spectrum," are forms of electronic communication, from radio to cellular phones to PCS, personal communications systems, to satellite transmissions. They range from 550 kilohertz (cycles per second) all the way up to twenty billion cycles, or 20 gigahertz, with cellular telephones in the 800-megahertz (eight hundred million) range.

The 1,460 cell-phone licenses were awarded by lottery, but many of the winners just turned around and sold their federal franchises to existing companies for a fortune, an unfair and wasteful program.

I wrote in 1992 that the government had to change its policy. That happened in 1994 when the FCC smartened up, under pressure. A policy of auctioning off the airwaves to the highest bidder was put in, with better-than-expected revenues.

In the four years since, FCC spectrum auctions have awarded more than forty-three hundred licenses in nine different wireless and satellite categories.

The take? TWENTY-THREE BILLION DOLLARS. The PCS hand-held miniature telephones, a modern version of the Dick Tracy receivers, were the winners, bringing in the majority of the money.

This was a big win for the taxpayer, for which I take some of the credit.

NEWSLETTERS

One of the longest-running governmental scams is the "newsletters" mailed to virtually every home in America by our members of Congress.

These "educational" mailings are actually reelection gambits that promote the representative along with his picture and what he's supposedly doing on behalf of his constituents, most of which ends up just costing them a pretty penny.

The newsletters themselves are quite expensive. In the typical House district of 585,000 people, there are generally 250,000 households on the mailing list. Many Americans think the congressional postage bill is *free* because the representative has the franking privilege. But that's only a convenience so that each piece doesn't have to be stamped. The congressman has to pay the U.S. Postal Service like any other citizen—about thirteen cents per piece, money that comes out of his allowance, which naturally, comes out of your pocket.

Each House member has a maximum franking allowance, which averages $109,000 each per year. Cumulatively, the postage bill of the House is almost $30 million a year, at least 90 percent of which is spent on mass mailings. In addition, there is the cost of printing these newsletters, or some $20 million more.

In the Senate, which does less of this nonsense, each senator has a $50,000-a-year mailing allowance, or an additional $5 million. That means more than $50 million a year is spent by Congress on these propaganda missives, money thrown down the waste drain. Voters get more information, and a little less slanted, on the nightly news.

"Congressional franking represents a form of public financing—but for incumbents only," says David Keating of the National Taxpayers Union.

When I first wrote about it in 1992, I had three complaints. One was the cost of the printing. The second was the cost of the mailing. The third was the fact that they were mailed so close to election day that they should be considered campaign brochures paid for with campaign funds, not our tax money.

Naturally, I suggested that all newsletters should be eliminated. But they haven't been.

What has happened since 1992? In 1993 Senator Connie Mack (R., FL) tried to stop the program by offering legislation that would eliminate the use of public funds for unsolicited mailings by Congress. He pointed out that 95 percent of franked mail is used for purposes other than answering constituent mail and is just another way for politicians to protect their jobs.

The vote to kill his amendment was close, but Mack lost forty-eight to forty-seven, and the taxpayers with him.

The House finally admitted that too heavy a load of newsletters was going out just before election. Finally, in September 1996, they decided that no "mass mailings" (i.e., newsletters) could be mailed within the period ninety days prior to election, either primary or general. This is somewhat helpful, but newsletters still come into our homes almost around the calendar.

To make congressmen's newsletters seem less partial and self-centered (even if they are), Congress has put in new rules. "Personally phrased references" such as "I" or "me" should not be overused, the Franking Commission rule book says. How often is too much? Not "more than eight times a page," they answer with a straight face. In an eight-page brochure that's sixty-four times.

The same is true of their vanity. Photos in which the member appears can't be used more than two times per page, or sixteen times in an eight-page newsletter—more than in any respectable campaign brochure.

Neither should newsletters seem too partisan, Congress warns. Their party affiliation can only be mentioned two times per page, or again, sixteen times. How much more partisan can you be?

The only reasonable requirement put in by the House is that the newsletter bear the following disclaimer:

"This mailing was prepared, published and mailed at taxpayer expense."

This makes eminent sense, but members can print this line in type as small as seven points, which makes it almost invisible to the older eye.

The solution? Quite obvious. The House and the Senate should pass a joint resolution to prohibit any mass mailings by members, except for one last one to boast that they have just saved the citizens' hard-earned money.

Until that day comes, this is a $50 million annual defeat for the taxpayers.

FOREST SERVICE—MORE CORPORATE WELFARE

Long before we realized that there was a category called "corporate welfare," I showed that the U.S. Forest Service was in the business of providing sweetheart deals for American lumber companies—at the expense of the taxpayer.

The Forest Service's holdings strain the imagination. They own 9 percent of the United States, a land mass of 192 million acres, larger than all of the New England states *combined*. One can just imagine the vast resources of timber that sit in their (our) woodlands.

It's a massive operation. In 1935, when the forest holdings were about the same size, it had four thousand employees. And today? Almost forty thousand.

What these people do for business is sell our lumber to private wood-products companies, which is not a bad idea. But they do it at a loss. Instead of making money on our natural resources, they have arranged to soak our forests in red ink.

In 1990 their budget was approximately the same as now, about $3.3 billion. Their receipts from the sale of lumber were $1.37 billion, money used to offset the huge deficit in paying for the bloated manpower. But over the years, from 1990 to 1996, the volume of trees harvested has continually gone down. In 1992 the income dropped to $1.1 billion, then down to $609 million in 1996, a sign of a program run by poor businessmen—i.e., government officials.

There are several reasons for the failure, one of which is pure corporate welfare. That's the building and maintenance of roads by the federal government so that the wood-products companies can come and buy the lumber, often at a discount. The government maintains the largest road network in the world in these forests.

How large? Believe it or not, 379,000 miles of roads, enough to stretch from New York to Los Angeles *120 times*, and eight times larger than the entire interstate network. The capital cost of the roads is in the billions, plus $136 million a year for new ones, and $77 million for maintenance, a total of $213 million per year, much of which the lumber companies should be paying. And would be, if not for the lumber lobby in Washington.

There are other *big* problems in this agency, according to the General Accounting Office. They include using oral bids to sell the lumber instead of sealed bids, which loses us $56 million a year. There is that ever-present "spotted owl" problem, which has cut down logging in the Pacific Northwest.

And perhaps most important is poor management, which over the latest six-year period has reduced the volume of board feet cut by 65 percent, the receipts by 55 percent, and the amount of money given back to the Treasury to cover their deficit by 85 percent.

In summary, "The Inspector General [of Agriculture, which runs the Forest Service] reported that, overall, the Forest Service could not determine for what purposes $215 million of its $3.4 billion in operating and program funds were spent." The General Accounting Office adds that "the Forest Service has also made little progress in holding its managers accountable for their performance."

This is a daily, continuing defeat for the American taxpayer. What more can I say?

CONGRESSIONAL PERKS

In 1992 members of the House and Senate wallowed in gifts, luncheons, dinners, handed out freely and openly by lobbyists. So bad was the situation that members went on free golf and fishing trips, with their spouses, all expenses paid, to Florida, California, even the Caribbean, without batting an eyelash of conscience. So they were in the pay of corporations. What of it?

They could even accept cash from lobbyists, and many did.

They were permitted to sponge as much as $250 per year in cash from each lobbyist, a sum that could add up to many thousands. Freebie meals could cost as much as $100 each, which amount *was not deducted* from their $250 allowance.

It was pig heaven, with a continuous flow of tickets to ball games, gifts at Christmas, or gifts whenever.

In *The Government Racket* I exposed much of this and asked for change, which eventually did come. In the House, Representatives Chris Shays (R., CT) and Linda Smith (R., WA) finally appealed to the conscience of their colleagues and passed a rule, effective 1996, cutting out *all* gifts, luncheons, dinners, trips—zilch—to House members.

In the Senate, Paul Wellstone (D., MN) pushed through legislation basically doing the same, except that senators held out for the last vestige of personal pork. They can still accept anything, especially a lunch or dinner, if it costs less than $50. That enables them to still freeload, but at less expensive restaurants.

That $50 barrier created another wonderful loophole that enabled senators to receive tickets to hockey and basketball games, and many senators have jumped through it. Lobbyists love to hand out tickets to members and their staffs for the games of the Washington Capitals hockey team and the NBA Wizards. Even though the tickets usually cost more than $50, the Senate Ethics Committee (you should excuse the expression) has decided that they qualify as $50 items on the basis of "value"—making a mockery of the gift rules.

House members chafed at their loss of freebie luncheons and finally, after three years, in 1999, gave in to common congressional temptation. They matched the Senate and reinstated the $50 gift allowance, which is bringing them back, en masse, to Washington's restaurants accompanied by their favorite lobbyists.

House members are also turning the tables. They now throw

fund-raising lunches for lobbyists and have their campaign fund pick up the tab. "It's ludicrous to think that a free dinner will buy off a member, but that a $5,000 check won't," says government professor Ronald Shaiko at American University.

You can't hold a good congressman down when perks are involved. They can also go to "well-attended events" such as dinners and luncheons for a group of members and staff. And the lobbyist-funded "fact-finding" trips, which take members all over the world, are still considered ethical.

Perks come and go in the House, and the killing of a few privileges gets more publicity than it deserves. The members recently lost a charming, if ridiculous, perk. For the last fifty years, twice a day, a bucket of fresh ice was automatically hand-delivered to each member's office, an opportunity to make mint juleps to ward off the oppressive heat of Washington summers.

The cost? A cool $1 million.

Now with air-conditioning, it was decided that the Iceman Goeth. (The perk still lives on as long as you *call and ask* for a bucket!) But other perk traditions have stood the test of time, and criticism.

One hallowed privilege, perhaps the most beloved of all, is a special parking spot reserved for members of Congress near the terminals at both Ronald Reagan Airport (once "National") and Dulles International. There has been one change, however. Until recently, the sign said that the space was reserved for members of Congress, justices of the Supreme Court, and cabinet officers.

Howls went up that the perk was blatant special privilege, the kind of advantage not available to taxpaying citizens.

What happened?

The parking perk stayed as is, but the sign was changed. Now it just says that the space is for "authorized" personnel.

The howls of protest have slowed the order of some House congressional perkers, but their appetite seems insatiable. According to the Association of Concerned Taxpayers and other sources, the following perks, among others, are still in place:

1. Members receive an untalked-about $3,000 housing deduction off their federal income taxes.

2. At tax time, the IRS sets up special shops for members in each House and Senate office building to help members and staff fill out their forms 1040.

3. They pay no D.C. sales taxes on items purchased in the Capitol building.

4. Even if they live in the District of Columbia, they (and two of their top staffers) are exempt from paying the high D.C. income taxes.

5. The National Gallery lends original paintings to members to decorate their offices.

6. There is a special office to wrap packages, free of charge, for members and senior staffers.

7. Both the House and Senate have a staff of photographers who take pictures of members and visiting constituents, then send them out, all free of charge.

8. Special shops in the House and Senate buildings frame pictures—from ordinary snapshots to huge posters—for members at no cost.

9. On defeat or retirement, members are allowed to take home their taxpayer-paid desk and chair as souvenirs of their days in Washington, at a nominal fee.

10. Members and staff are frequent-fliers par excellence. They fly around the country and to and from home on

government-paid airline tickets, for which they receive bonus miles. Executive branch employees can't keep frequent-flier miles for themselves, but Congress has arranged for members and their staffs to keep, and personally use, the taxpayer-paid airline freebies.

11. Seventy-nine senators with the longest seniority each have a special hideaway office off the Senate floor and Capitol hallways. This is in addition to their regular suite of offices.

12. When members and staff use their personal cars for business, they are reimbursed at a higher mileage rate than ordinary taxpayers can claim on their IRS returns.

13. Long-distance phone services are available free of charge to members and their senior staffs. At home they can tap into the freebie telephone with a special code.

14. The Library of Congress operates a lending-library service for members and staff. There are no fines for overdue books, and thousands of books go unreturned each year.

15. Members have great opportunity to provide patronage jobs for friends, including the hiring of young pages.

16. Leaders in the House and Senate have free limos along with chauffeurs, most of whom are Capitol police taken away from their regular duties to drive congressional brass.

Do all these perks still exist?

As we have seen in the *omertà* of silence in the case of the House and Senate recording studios, Congress is somewhat paranoid about revealing, or even discussing, its perks—somewhat reminiscent of the Soviet *nomenklatura* during the old, bad days. When the above list was given to the House Administration Committee to check it for accuracy, a spokesperson said that they *never* comment on the privileges of House members!

There are perks lurking everywhere—see Chapters 26 and 27, Radio Ads and Recording Studios, and the sections in this Part Two on Newsletters and especially Congressional Retirement, the mother of them all.

Both houses of Congress, for instance, had subsidized barbershops and beauty salons for years. Finally, reacting to criticism, in 1995 the House privatized their operation, saving over $100,000 a year.

But the Senate has held out, and their government-subsidized barbershop and beauty salon—with a staff of some seventeen—loses $360,000 a year. There are no underpaid workers here. The barbers get $62,000 a year, and the receptionists $42,000, in the style of Uncle Sam's attitude toward Other People's Money—mine and yours.

This litany of perks costs money, but it will not bankrupt the U.S. Treasury. What it does is set up a hidden mindset among members of Congress that they are somehow very special—some kind of *Ubermenschen*—and somehow operating above and beyond the concerns of their constituents. It is a slowly crippling psychic disease that ends in indifference to the true needs of the American people for a smaller, more efficient, less wasteful government.

We have had a small victory in the perk reforms of 1995, but the battle continues.

What should we do?

The answer is obvious. *All congressional perks should be abolished. Not only will we save money, but it will help remind members of the struggles in the real world.*

There is one peculiar perk that members apparently take for granted, which would be considered a symptom of a clinical condition in a saner environment than the Beltway.

What is that sublime perk?

All the elevators in the Capitol building are constructed to be self-operated. But instead, each one has a federal-employee elevator operator pressing the buttons for the members.

Was that designed just to see how much money could be wasted? Or is it a perk to spare members the effort of thrusting out their index fingers?

We'll never know.

PART THREE

BLUEPRINT FOR THE TWENTY-FIRST CENTURY

How to Redesign the Government and Save a Fortune in the Process

All the waste, fraud, poor planning, and ignorance that now dominate the federal government, in virtually every agency, need not exist. Not only do we need public protest to stop it, but someone has to *design* a total reform of the operation so that it functions more intelligently and with greater efficiency.

It requires, among other things, a fail-safe method of cutting out wasteful programs before they become entrenched, and to eliminate them once they have proved unworthy.

At one point in 1993, Senator John Glenn, then head of a Senate Committee on Governmental Operations, had announced such a goal, including a restructuring of the cabinet and the elimination of many malfunctioning agencies. By coincidence, I was testifying before the Senate that day and met privately with the senator beforehand, a meeting in which he outlined some excellent ideas for government overhaul.

But only minutes later, in the midst of the hearing, Leon Panetta, then head of the Office of Management and Budget, testified that Vice President Al Gore was himself investigating government waste and inefficiency and would soon come up with a plan called "reinventing government." (That report, "Reinventing Government," has since come out and has proved to be a minuscule, insignificant "reform" of a badly askew government.)

Since Gore was working on the project, Panetta said, he thought Senator Glenn would be well advised to drop his investigation of the executive branch and his plans for restructuring the government. When I testified, just a few minutes later, the senator asked me what I thought. I responded that asking Vice President Gore to probe the government was like asking the foxes to police the henhouse. I said the senator should go ahead with his investigation, full steam.

That night I appeared on Tom Snyder's show on CNBC. I assured Snyder that Glenn was on the case and good things were going to happen. He sneered at my optimism, and of course, was proven correct. Glenn dropped his attempt at reform and joined the White House "reinventing government" team.

Now, with your permission, I will attempt my own rather radical restructuring of the Washington operation, with emphasis on clarity, cutting of costs, and elimination of duplication, waste, and fraud. Should we ever accomplish such a citizen revolution, it would finally provide American taxpayers with a central government they can afford and be proud of.

Follow me, please, into the uncharted waters of true reform.

In enumerating just some of the government waste, as we have done, we should look at that unfortunate situation as a *symptom* rather than as a cause of our problem.

The problem is that the federal government is chaotic, a series of patchwork programs without a significant plan or even, in many cases, a raison d'être. The government in Washington has grown over the years, piece by piece, agency by agency, program by program, in answer to perceived needs of the moment—whether depression, war, poverty, or other real, or imagined, crises. Except for its limited constitutional duties, the federal government is mainly an ad hoc, patched-together, dysfunctional operation.

To make matters worse, Congress and the presidents are addicted to using our tax money for programs the people do not approve of, or often are not even aware of, thus ever expanding an already entrenched bureaucracy.

There is also an inordinate interest in special interests that are vocal and armed with lobbyists and heavy campaign chests. The actions of Congress are too often dictated by self-interest (reelection) and by the dispensing of funds (pork, for instance) that are aimed at votes rather than necessity.

Even when congressional legislation does make sense, the executive branch does a poor job carrying out the laws by setting up multiple, inefficient, expensive bureaucracies. They then try to explain away their failure with clever rhetoric aimed at mollifying the electorate. In its relation with its citizens, the federal government operates more as a corner-cutting ad agency than as a truthful trustee.

The tax structure, being based on income, is distorted and excessive and in great need of radical reform. At no time in our history has such a large percentage of the gross domestic product gone to taxes, both federal and state, a crushing burden rationalized by propaganda about surpluses and the false need to maintain such large governments.

From a $200 billion budget in 1973, federal spending has now reached $2 trillion, a tenfold increase. *If the cost had just followed the rise in inflation, the government budget today would be only half its present gargantuan size.*

Can much be done to change the situation?

Yes, but it will require not just piecemeal reform such as

glib "reinventing," but a systematic restructuring of the entire federal government.

Many had hoped that the "revolution" of 1994, which had brought in the first Republican Congress in forty-two years, would begin the rebuilding process. There have been some minor changes, as we've seen in Part Two. But in essence, the waste has continued unabated. In fact, in the three years from 1995 to 1997, nondefense spending *rose* by $183 billion. The only major cuts have been in defense, which may yet prove to be a fool's paradise.

Still, it will not profit us to become pessimistic. Americans should not easily accept the fact that we will always be over-taxed to support a government that is not only antipragmatic, but anti-intellectual as well.

Instead, all well-intentioned rational citizens should redouble their efforts to bring sanity to Washington. What is needed is a carefully constructed *plan* that is neither mean-spirited nor childishly spendthrift.

Here, then, is my practical, no-nonsense way to reorganize the federal government so that the nation can once again feel secure that Washington is fulfilling the vision of the Founding Fathers.

THE CABINET

In the beginning there were only five cabinet agencies. In 1789, after the inauguration of President Washington, three high-level agencies were formed: the Department of Foreign Affairs, which later became the State Department, the War Department, and the Treasury Department. A postmaster general and an attorney general were also named but did not achieve cabinet status until later.

A Department of the Navy was established in 1798, but no

other cabinet post was created until 1849, when, as we moved westward, the Home Department, later the Department of the Interior, was established. In 1889, in recognition of agriculture as the main industry of the nation, the Department of Agriculture was set up. In 1903 the Department of Commerce and Labor was created; it would be split into two agencies in 1913.

For thirty-four years, until after World War II, there were no new cabinet agencies, which then totaled eight, counting the postmaster general, who is no longer in the cabinet.

From that net of seven, the size of the cabinet has now doubled to fourteen.

In 1947 we added the Department of Defense, a successor to the War Department. In 1953 the grab bag called the Department of Health, Education and Welfare (HEW), now Health and Human Services (HHS), was established. In 1965 we added the Department of Housing and Urban Development (HUD) as part of the Great Society, followed by the Department of Transportation in 1966. In 1979 HHS took on its new name as the Office of Education split off to become its own cabinet-level agency as the Department of Education. The last of the fourteen was the Department of Veterans Affairs, formed in 1989 from the lower-echelon Veterans Administration.

Today there is further talk of raising the U.S. trade representative to cabinet level, along with the Environmental Protection Agency.

The cabinet cries out for reorganization, both in size and structure. A proper reform would begin with one given: we need those slots that were established in George Washington's term—State, Treasury, Justice, and War, now Defense. In addition to those four, our reorganization should return the cabinet close to the size it was at the end of World War II, a total of nine.

A new smaller, more rational cabinet would look like this, beginning with these five agencies:

- Department of State
- Department of the Treasury
- Department of Defense
- Department of Justice
- Department of Natural Resources

This new fifth slot would combine all activities that involve natural resources. It would include the present Department of the Interior, and would take the Forest Service out of Agriculture, where it does not belong, and fold in both the Department of Agriculture and the Department of Energy.

The Department of Agriculture does not need to be a separate cabinet agency. America has fewer than one million full-time farmers, most of whom are "aggie" graduates and more knowledgeable than most county agricultural agents. The size of the USDA is outlandish, with sixty-five thousand non-Forest Service people, and over ten thousand offices around the country, or one for every one hundred farmers. One office in Texas handles only fifteen farmers.

Agriculture as a cabinet department is an archaic overhang from the days when farming was the main occupation in the nation. Today, more people and more money are involved in the computer industry, yet we do not have a Department of Computers. Further, the primary activity of the department—farm subsidies and forced conservation to keep up prices—is now being phased out, which makes the department a governmental dinosaur. (The remaining subsidies, such as those for peanuts and sugar, should be discontinued immediately.)

We need only to maintain agricultural research, much of which is done as federal-state partnerships in the land grant colleges of the Midwest. An Office of Agricultural Research should be set up as part of the new Department of Natural Resources.

The Department of Energy is also an anomaly in modern government, and would be folded into the new Department of Natural Resources. It manufactures nuclear weapons, researches solar-driven cars, and helps pay for the heating bills of the indigent aged. Its nuclear activity should be returned to a new Atomic Energy Commission, and its other activities put into the appropriate cabinet groups.

The other four cabinet slots would include:

THE DEPARTMENT OF INDUSTRY AND LABOR
Combine Labor and Commerce into One New Department

The functions of the present Department of Labor and Department of Commerce, both having to do with gainful work and production, should be combined, as they once were. In this way, both workers and management can be brought closer together.

One example of failure that can be corrected by joining these two is our present job-training program, which costs us $25 billion a year but fails to train many people for work. Through a combined new cabinet office, we could establish a valid apprentice program such as they have in Germany. Youngsters in their third year of high school apprentice part-time to a corporation in everything from metallurgy to computer programming while they continue attending school part-time. They receive a nominal $5,000 to $8,000 a year for their work until they graduate and become journeymen at three times that salary. The head of the Hanover Chamber of Industry has given that collaborative effort credit for Germany's postwar success.

At present, in theory, the two cabinet agencies are antagonistic rather than synergistic. That should change.

DEPARTMENT OF WELFARE

A New Agency to Eliminate Duplication in Helping the Poor; Downgrade and Incorporate the Department of Education

As we have seen, the eighty-one welfare programs in America cost more than the Defense Department, and are operated out of six different cabinet agencies, including the IRS, which handles Earned Income Tax Credit, and HHS, which handles Medicaid, and the Department of Agriculture, which handles food stamps. Instead all programs will be placed in the new Department of Welfare, which will be responsible for feeding, housing, and educating the poor.

Its first job will be to computerize all its functions so that Washington will know what is happening to the $400 billion a year in welfare (three-fourths federal) and how much welfare—in terms of benefits and programs—any individual is receiving.

Just that coordination will save billions, for Congress should establish limits on aid to any one poor family or individual, something they cannot do with the present lack of knowledge. Perhaps most important, the eighty-one programs can be cut down to a half dozen.

This new department will also take over the functions of the Department of Education in such areas as help to disadvantaged children and community colleges in poor areas. Except for those functions, the Department of Education serves little purpose and should be closed. (Student loans should be maintained and set up under a separate independent agency.)

As Americans know, education is a local and state function. Washington now pays only 7 percent of the elementary and secondary education bill. That money should now be sent to the states in the form of education grants to be used as they see fit, without federal intervention.

DEPARTMENT OF HEALTH
Turn HHS into a Purely Medical Organization

The present Department of Health and Human Services is another grab-bag cabinet agency that should be reformed. With all its welfare services shifted to the new Department of Welfare, it can be an exclusively medical and health agency that seeks to improve medical care and extend longevity. It would be renamed the Department of Health.

It should be headed by a physician, who will administer Medicare, Medicaid, the surgeon general's office, public health, the communicable disease office in Atlanta, the National Institutes of Health, and all other medical-research activities of the federal government.

Stripped of its current multiple functions, it can concentrate on the health of the nation.

DEPARTMENT OF URBAN, SUBURBAN, AND RURAL AFFAIRS
Fold HUD into This Broader Agency; Incorporate the Department of Transportation

This is the last of the nine cabinet areas I have proposed.

This new agency will take over the work of HUD (Housing and Urban Development) and combine it with the discontinued Department of Transportation, a vital aspect of life in all three covered areas.

In the world of giveaways, the cities and rural areas have been heavily on the dole since the 1960s. But the suburbs have been ignored. This new agency will even the score. It will also include the Federal Highway Administration, so that roads crisscrossing the suburbs will be included.

This completes the consolidation of fourteen of the cabinet agencies into nine. The Department of Veterans Affairs, which was only recently elevated to cabinet level, will be returned to the status of an independent agency. It will continue its work as is, but we should be cognizant of the fact that its scope is being reduced daily as the largest group of veterans, the sixteen million men and women from World War II, continue to pass away, and will be mainly gone within a decade.

Since the 1960s, a host of independent agencies, a kind of little cabinet, have arisen, most of which must also be cut back.

THE OVERSIZED LITTLE CABINET

These independent or semiautonomous agencies—from the Bureau of Alcohol, Tobacco, and Firearms to the U.S. Fish and Wildlife Service—are some fifty strong and need to be pared down. In the past decade, the only significant one that has been eliminated—after much infighting—is the Interstate Commerce Commission.

Those that should now be *closed* include:

- Appalachian Regional Commission
- Agency for International Development
- Export-Import Bank of the U.S.
- Farm Credit Administration
- Federal Railroad Administration
- Federal Transit Administration
- Maritime Administration
- Overseas Private Investment Corporation
- Small Business Administration

PROGRAMS THAT SHOULD BE ELIMINATED

Many programs that spend a great deal of money without visible results are not autonomous, but are part of larger cabinet agencies. Some will be eliminated in the cabinet reorganization I have proposed, but others will linger on until Congress closes them down.

My list of programs that should be closed includes:

- Essential Air
- Federal support for political conventions
- Federal grants for mass transit
- AmeriCorps program
- Office of Former Speakers
- Rural Utilities Service
- Moratorium on construction of all new federal buildings
- Sale of the four Power Marketing agencies that provide taxpayer-subsidized electricity to some communities
- Moratorium on the purchase of new land by the federal government, which now costs $200 million a year at up to $50,000 an acre
- Market Access Program for food companies
- Federal subsidies for the merchant marine
- Advanced Technology Program
- Federal subsidies to the Big Three car companies
- Ethanol tax subsidies
- Demonstration projects for highways
- Community Development Block Grants

- Economic Development Initiatives in HUD
- Eliminating government-employee use of military golf courses
- International enterprise funds
- Metric program
- Peanut and sugar programs
- Eliminate disaster relief for private organizations and recreational facilities
- SSI pensions for disabled children
- Universal Service Fund
- Virtually free land patents under the Mining Law of 1872
- U.S. Forest Service roads being built for convenience of lumber companies

ANTISUBSIDY ACT

Much of the preceding list includes what is called "corporate welfare," 125 programs that cost us an estimated $75 billion a year. To eliminate that waste in every facet of the federal government, we need to pass an "Antisubsidy Act," which would make it illegal for the federal government to spend even $1 to subsidize any private business organization.

Rather than cull out that waste one program at a time, this act would accomplish it all in one bill.

DUPLICATION AND OVERLAP

One of the heinous sins of the federal government is its continuous duplication of programs in competing agencies.

As we have seen, there are now 127 programs for teenagers in *fifteen different agencies*, costing some $4 billion a year.

The same process takes place everywhere in Washington.

Education is now handled by twelve different agencies. Coastal water control is handled by four; wetlands by five. Native Americans are being aided by thirteen different groups. Even childhood immunizations have four funding sources. Three major agencies—the Public Health Service, Medicaid, and the Department of Agriculture—spend $9 billion a year to reduce infant mortality.

Fourteen different agencies compete in the arena of job training, which "boasts" some 160 different programs that cost $25 billion a year. (New legislation aims to trim down the amount of duplication.)

The reason, of course, is the *sovereign delusion* of many agencies that they are at the core of government, and that by extending their operations as widely as possible, they are performing a public service.

Physical fitness and healthy diets for Americans came out of several Washington sources: the Food and Drug Administration, School Health Education Activities, the President's Council on Physical Fitness, and the National Institutes of Health Exercise and Fitness Research, plus the Department of Labor's home nutrition program.

Environmental protection is split up in ten agencies in addition to the EPA.

The government's concern for children provides a grand opportunity for wasteful overlap. Those programs now cost us over $100 billion a year, but have no central focus. The Congressional Budget Office recently stated that by consolidating only five childhood programs started since 1989, the government would save $270 million a year.

The answer to waste through duplication lies in both the

executive branch and Congress. The first step is for the OMB to program a central computer so that we can instantly learn how many agencies, for example, are handling education or any other program.

A central task force on duplication and overlap should be set up jointly by the White House and Congress to track this, then report back to the public, with recommendations on which duplicating programs to cut out.

The goal should be simple: ONE MISSION, ONE AGENCY.

But even before the executive gets involved, Congress must plan not to legislate duplicating programs. Let's see how that can be managed.

CONGRESS

In a parliamentary system—which we do not have—much of the ills of legislation can be eliminated before they begin.

Since the Parliament in other nations is both the legislative and executive branches of government, there is less opportunity for duplication and waste. A minister responsible for a legislative agenda is also the man who will administer the program. Hence there is less interest in doing the same thing over and over again.

In the American Congress, things are quite different. The laws they pass are not administered by them but by the executive branch. There is little discipline on members of Congress whose interest in legislation is often motivated by the desire for publicity. Too often there is no one to stop them from proposing an unneeded and duplicative bill.

No one needs a 161st job-training bill—except the member who has his eye on reelection. There is no parliamentary "minister" to tell him to forget it. In this case, the *separation* of powers is a detriment, for the executive merely sets up a new bureaucracy as required by law.

Since we do not and will never have a parliamentary system, we need a new mechanism to stop unneeded and duplicating legislation—such as a 128th teenage bill. The answer is quite simple: .

Congress should set up a screening committee, which will report back on which bills have already been passed on the subject and exist in some form. This will require an expert computer system with software programmed to go back at least a half century. It can then print out all the similar bills, and where in the bureaucracy a similar program is in effect—in which executive agency and under which cabinet jurisdiction.

To accomplish this, Congress needs a "Committee on New Legislation," empowered, both in the House and the Senate, to do this screening job.

This group should then work with the executive branch, which will develop its own screen. Through this combined effort, perhaps half the legislation now passed in Congress— much of it for self-aggrandizement—will be eliminated at its source.

Other reforms needed to make Congress work more efficiently include:

1. Elimination of franking for mass mailings, radio ads, and subsidized prices in the House or Senate recording studios.

2. Elimination of all perks for members of Congress.

3. Reductions in congressional retirement plans, lowering the amount paid with taxpayer money. Changes in eligibility should make it impossible for members to draw their earned pension until they reach sixty-two, instead of the present fifty years of age.

4. Elimination of chauffeurs and limos for party leaders since they are not elected by the whole Congress. Only the Speaker of the House should be eligible for such perks.

5. Removal of ex-members' privilege of walking onto the floor of Congress. Some five hundred are now lobbyists and use this perk to advance their new businesses.

6. Legislation to make it illegal for former members to ever lobby Congress.

7. New rules to regulate junkets on military aircraft. No spouse accompanying the member should be permitted to fly on taxpayer money. In such cases, the member will have to pay the cost of transport by military aircraft. Further, a congressional screening committee should decide beforehand if the junket is necessary. They should publicly announce their decision along with the expected cost to taxpayers.

8. All legislation should be passed with a "sunset" provision, which would cut off the program after a number of years. Under a sunset provision, if the legislated program is successful, it can be renewed by Congress. If not, it will automatically die.

9. There are over one thousand district offices of the House alone. Each congressman should be allowed only one district office, plus the use of an 800 number. This will save staff and office costs.

10. The number of staff employees in Congress is now thirty thousand. It should be reduced by one third, mainly by cutting House members' staffs from eighteen (plus four part-time) to one dozen, and Senators' staffs from forty to twenty-five. Committee staffs, as well, should be reduced by the same one third.

11. The committees in Congress now number over two hundred. This makes it virtually impossible for most members to attend hearings. The committees should be consolidated to one hundred or fewer.

12. Members of Congress are bogged down by constituent service, which gains them friends and voters, but interferes with their job of legislating. (Many members now vote on bills they haven't read.) Instead of constituent service by members, a central congressional ombudsman service should be set up to handle all requests, complaints, etc., from constituents.

13. Committee chairmen should be limited to a term of four years in office.

14. The same should be true of the Speaker of the House.

15. Ethical disputes in Congress should not be handled by other members in an Ethics Committee, but by a special panel of retired federal judges named on a bipartisan basis by Congress.

PORK

Congress has other problems, the most serious of which is pork, the fatty sustenance of many shortsighted members, who love to boast to naive constituents that they have brought home the bacon.

As I have already mentioned, only Congress can stop this giant drain of tax money. All both houses need to do is to pass my "Antipork Law," which has two basic segments:

1. No member of the twenty-six appropriations committees in the House or Senate, or any of their subcommittees, may

propose or add an extra expenditure to a bill in which funds will go to the member's home district.

2. No member may arrange to have some other member propose the same for him. If there is any such exchange, it will be considered unethical behavior and result in automatic expulsion from the House or Senate.

Special attention has to be paid to the activities of the Transportation Committees, the Community Development Block Grant, and the Economic Development Initiatives of HUD, where a good part of pork exists. However, it is also spread out and infects *all* activities of the government.

My antipork rule in Congress could save America upward of $15 billion a year.

PRESIDENTIAL PRIMARIES

Americans tend to accept nonsensical political procedures as reasonable as long as they are traditional.

That especially applies to our quadrennial presidential primaries. Nothing in the political world makes less sense than the way we choose the nominees for our two major political parties.

Three quarters of the states hold public primaries, each with its own rules. In California, only Republicans can vote in the Republican primary. In others, like New Hampshire, both Republicans and Independents can vote. In some, including Wisconsin, there are "open primaries," a strange phenomenon in which everyone, even opposition Democrats, can intrude in the Republican primary, and vice versa.

Delegates are chosen by different formulas from state to state. New Hampshire, the first and most famous primary, divides the vote into a proportionate number of delegates for each candidate who gets at least 10 percent of the total. But big California, with 165 Republican delegates, gives all the delegates to the top vote getter—even if he wins by only one vote.

In caucuses such as those in Iowa, about one in six party members show up in someone's playroom or in a schoolhouse and argue, then vote. *But the irony of the Iowa caucus, which comes before New Hampshire, is that the vote doesn't count at all in choosing delegates.*

In 1996, by taking the caucuses seriously, five of the nine Republicans felt effectively wiped out even though not a single Iowa delegate was chosen that night. Later on, a state party convention chose its twenty-five delegates regardless of how the people voted.

Our presidential primaries are all absolute nonsense. But the parties, the public, and the media take it all quite seriously—especially the first primary vote in New Hampshire held in February.

In terms of real power, that state has more influence on the presidential selection process than others, and more than it should have if logic reigned. The potency of the New Hampshire primary cannot be overestimated. Nor is it any way sensible.

Every four years, a squadron of presidential hopefuls—some of whom have been semiresidents in the state for over a year—do retail campaigning, one person at a time in supermarkets, at breakfast in a diner, or right on the street, trying to convince stubborn Yankees that they and no one else should sit in the Oval Office.

New Hampshire is always first in the primary sweepstakes, which is a highly debatable concept to begin with. The northeastern state has many virtues, especially the fact that they have no sales tax or state income tax. But it is totally unrepresentative of America in most ways. It is geographically small, only nine thousand square miles. It is sparsely populated, with a total of 1.1 million people, about half as many as the Bronx. Its largest city, Manchester, has fewer than one hundred thousand people. Its population is skewed, with 98 percent being white.

But this proud little state, with about a third of 1 percent of the national population, often dictates who runs for president, or more accurately, who is eliminated from the selection process early on.

The latest conflict in this messy, unreasonable procedure is that several states have become angry at New Hampshire for being first, and are intent on beating them out for the national publicity. Louisiana decided they would vote before New Hampshire, and Delaware just four days afterward. *But this angered New Hampshire, which now forces candidates to pledge that they will not campaign in Louisiana or Delaware at the risk of not being allowed into the New Hampshire primary.*

Now California and New York, who used to hold their primaries as late as June when their votes were meaningless—the candidate having been all but formally chosen by that time—are eager to get into the act. They have moved their primaries up to March, just weeks after New Hampshire.

The entire presidential primary system is a fantasy the two parties have created to please themselves, and have falsely passed off as being rational, democratic, and a service to the people.

What should we do instead?

The answer is obvious. Choosing the party presidential nominees requires national, not state, primary elections held coast to coast.

A uniform national primary for presidential candidates would be held in the following way:

1. Only citizens registered in a particular party shall be able to vote in their party's primary. There will be no "open" or "crossover" primaries.

2. There will be no caucuses and no delegates chosen by state party conventions. Nor will there be any delegates to the presidential nominating convention chosen by state primaries.

3. There shall be a series of two national primary elections held throughout the country. In the first, *all* party candidates, no matter how many, will compete on the same day. The vote will be held the first Saturday in March.

4. If any of the candidates receives a *majority* of the votes, he will automatically be the candidate of his party. If no one receives a majority, there will be a runoff election in June in which only the *top two* vote getters will participate.

5. The candidate who wins that race will be the party's presidential candidate.

6. A national convention will be held in July to confirm the nominee and adopt a party platform (The party, not the taxpayers—as is the current policy—will pay for the usually gaudy political shindig.)

Robert M. La Follette, the progressive reformer who began the primary system in Wisconsin, was hopeful of creating a system in which the party bosses wouldn't handpick our Presidents. But the smoke-filled room held sway until 1952, when the New Hampshire primary chose Dwight D. Eisenhower over Robert Taft.

From then on, the bosses were replaced by a system with the appearance of democratic choice, but one marred by a maddening series of differing regulations, public primaries, caucuses, state conventions, conflicting dates, and true *chaos*.

Only a national primary, with one runoff, can cleanse the present primary system, just as La Follette eventually succeeded in breaking the power of many state political machines.

It will surely take national legislation to accomplish this, perhaps even a constitutional amendment. But choosing Presidents has become more vital than ever in the complex twenty-first century, and this reform is surely worth the effort.

TAXES: ELIMINATE THE INTERNAL REVENUE SERVICE

The burden of taxation is excessive in America, where some 38 percent of the gross domestic product goes into supporting governments of all kind. On the national level, taxation has reached an all-time high. Remedies, even from conservative legislators, are insufficient to change the picture.

Defender's of America's high tax structure like to point out that Europeans pay even higher taxes, which is a misleading, fatuous argument. In the welfare states of Western Europe, middle-class citizens receive virtually free medical care, inexpensive, sometimes free, university education, large unemployment insurance benefits over a long period of time, long vacations, tax-supported day care for children, plus an endless list of goodies. If we just add America's private medical costs of almost a trillion dollars a year to our present taxes, we become, in effect, one of the highest-taxed nations of the world.

The reason is that taxation is not market-based. Every time the White House or Congress has another pet project, the rates are ratcheted upward, often with lies to cover the reality. For example, Medicare taxes of 1.45 percent were once limited to the same ceiling as Social Security, but are now *unlimited*. That is, people must pay that percentage on their entire income. For self-employed people, that's an extra 2.7 percent. Then in 1993, the White House pushed through still larger increases in tax brackets.

The answer, of course, is to eliminate the income tax as the major source of revenue and substitute another system. The first step is for Congress to pass a law eliminating the income tax. A constitutional amendment is not necessary; the Sixteenth Amendment, which legalized the tax, need not be repealed. It stated only that Congress *shall have the power* to lay and collect taxes on income. It did not say it had to.

Further, a case can be made that the enforcement method of the income tax is a violation of the Fourth Amendment, which states:

"The right of the people to be secure in their persons, houses, papers and effects against unreasonable search and seizure shall not be violated."

Tell that constitutional guarantee to anyone who has been audited and who is commanded to bring in his private "papers" for examination by the IRS. Will the Fourth Amendment protect him from penalties or possible prosecution? Hardly.

Once Congress votes to eliminate the IRS, what will replace it?

Since there will be no IRS, the only possibility is a consumer tax, or as it is best known, a "national sales tax," which will be collected by the states, whose costs shall be reimbursed by Washington. Under my plan not all the revenue of the federal government need be raised by this tax. It will merely substitute for all monies taken in by Form 1040, which covers salaries, royalties, interest income, capital gains, and inheritances.

That frees almost all Americans from the need to file anything with anybody, along with freedom from personal intrusion, penalties, interest, and confiscations, plus the invasion of privacy outlawed by the Fourth Amendment.

Form 1040 raises less than $900 billion a year, which has to be replaced. We will keep the corporate tax intact for the present, along with the excise taxes and fees. To collect the needed amount will require a 13.5 percent national sales tax, but with an exemption for food, medical care, and housing. This will benefit the poor, who might also receive a full or partial refund of their regressive FICA tax.

If we choose to raise the sales tax to 20 percent, we could eliminate the employee's end of the FICA tax altogether. *That would mean that there would be no federal deduction of any kind from our paychecks.* (The employer's portion of the FICA would be retained.)

When I wrote *The Tax Racket* in 1995 and proposed this plan, I was accused of promoting pipe dreams. But since then we have had the revelations of the crude operation of the IRS. We have also seen a better tax-educated public understand that a market-based tax is less susceptible to being raised on a presidential or congressional whim. If too high a national sales tax results in cutting car sales, for example, Congress will hear a loud protest from industry. Mr. Ford has more clout in Washington than does Mr. Jones.

We have seen that a large portion of public opinion is now in favor of closing the Internal Revenue Service. The head of the House Ways and Means Committee, Bill Archer of Texas, is in favor of a national sales tax, and Representative Billy Tauzin is sponsoring legislation to make it a reality.

Continued pressure may well move the "pipe dream" of closing the IRS into reality, creating a new unprecedented prosperity in American history.

INITIATIVE AND REFERENDUM

Americans talk a good deal about "democracy," but often do little to improve it.

We read regularly about "propositions" being offered on the ballot in California and other states, but many people are not aware that this democratic privilege is not available to most citizens of the country.

Called the "Initiative," it enables citizens in twenty-six states to get petitions signed, then have a proposition for a tax reduction, or social change, placed on the ballot. In most cases, if citizens vote "Yes," it not only becomes law, but is incorporated into the state constitution.

Most of the states that have true Initiative laws are in the West. As pioneers moved westward they decided to eliminate big boss and professional politician rule as much as they could through the Initiative. By and large it is those states that have the superior democracies.

Politicians in the older Eastern states have resisted bringing in the Initiative, fearful that citizens would revolt against current tax levels, which in New York and Connecticut are the highest in the nation. In 1991, when Connecticut politicians put through the state's first-ever state income tax, public opinion was overwhelmingly against it, preferring the heavier sales tax. But the income tax was instituted in the absence of the Initiative, which would have eliminated it posthaste at the ballot box.

(In fact, I received a personal promise from Governor John Rowland, then running for his first term, that he would press to get the Initiative instituted in Connecticut. Not only did this promise prove to be hollow, I was even removed from a committee investigating its adoption.)

The answer is quite simple. We need a constitutional amendment that guarantees the right of Initiative for all citizens of the nation, in all 50 states. With the proper push that should be possible. Such an amendment requires the approval of thirty-six states—twenty-six of whom already have the Initiative.

Spreading democracy to all corners of the nation should be

a national priority. *In fact, I am amazed that citizens in the states without it have not demanded it, and punished professional politicians who stand in its way.*

REFERENDUM

Many developed nations leave to their citizens, rather than just to their legislatures, the decision on many major issues. For example, several nations had their citizens vote to approve the move into the European Union—which some then rejected.

The American Constitution did not grant citizens the right to "approve" or "reject" the work of Congress. But in the ideal democracy, voters would have that right on *major issues* that affect everyone, a right referred to as "Referendum."

For example, taxes are one area where citizens should have more say on the national scene. Rates, which are too high, change regularly (generally in favor of governments and against citizens) and make it difficult for citizens to arrange their economic life.

The perfect use of a Referendum would be to have a national vote whether we should maintain the present Internal Revenue income tax method, or switch to a national sales tax or some other form of non-income taxation. At present, American citizens are powerless in that debate, merely watching as members of Congress debate their future.

Other areas in which we might use the Referendum to extend democracy are war and peace, the composition of the cabinet—which keeps being extended irrationally—immigration, and other major issues.

Now that we are a mature democracy, it is time to consider not only the state-by-state Initiative, but a constitutional amendment (perhaps incorporated into the same one) to add a National

Referendum to those instruments of citizen participation that in the long run only enhance our democracy.

If we want to actually achieve the blessings of government by the people, we will insist on the Initiative and Referendum for everyone.

ESTABLISH AN INDEPENDENT
INSPECTOR GENERAL OF THE UNITED STATES

One of the gravest problems we face in controlling waste is that there is not one central place in government that can evaluate how much money is being thrown down the drain, and then exercise power to correct it.

Some investigators in the General Accounting Office could be tougher with the agencies they cover. But by and large, the GAO is the only bright spot that illuminates the executive branch's massive waste operation. Too often the agencies do what they please, the public be damned.

The GAO does a massive job of investigating, but since they are a branch of Congress, the executive branch usually ignores their recommendations, or *pretends* they are complying. Congress itself doesn't listen sufficiently to the GAO and appropriates more money for programs even when it has been proven that they are not working.

In the executive branch itself, each agency has an inspector general, who spends most of his or her time tracking down individual cases of fraud. That's valuable, but too often misses the larger picture of waste. By structure, the IGs can't step out too far in investigating because they report to the cabinet secretary or head of the agency. This inhibition makes it virtually impossible to delve into the hidden aspects of government waste, or even fraud on the part of the higher-ups. Few IGs want to lose their jobs by performing too courageously.

The system has to be changed, and I believe I know exactly how to accomplish it.

We need an independent organization, much as the Federal Reserve is independent, to regularly check up on the entire federal government—the executive, legislative, and judicial branches. It will be called the Office of the Inspector General of the United States. The organization will be headed by a person named by the President for a five-year term that overlaps elections, and will be confirmed by the Senate. His or her salary will equal that of the Vice President.

Like the Federal Reserve chairman, the national Inspector General will be beholden to no one, and will appoint an IG to each agency or department of government. *But unlike the present system, they will not report to the cabinet member or agency chief, but directly to the Inspector General of the United States.*

The job will be all-encompassing. The IG will check on fraud, all the way up the line, from agencies to Congress to the White House. He will operate on tips regarding waste from whistle-blowers, journalists, material from the GAO, leads from congressmen and citizens. These leads will be fleshed out with independent research by his large staff of investigators. He will have subpoena power, subject to court approval.

The IG will issue quarterly reports on waste, fraud, and abuse. Since he is independent, there is no province of government that will be exempt from his purview.

The monthly reports will go to every branch of government and will be released to the press, and to any citizen who wants to purchase a copy at a nominal sum. In addition, the inspector general will testify before Congress four times a year.

The present IG system has value but is limited in scope and totally beholden to the cabinet or agency branch. The personnel in the present IG offices will not be fired. They will be folded into the new Office of the Inspector General of the United States, but rotated out of their present agency to new positions.

The person who occupies this new inspector general spot will inherit enormous prestige, power, and responsibility, and could contribute more to efficient government than anyone in the nation's history.

And incidentally, I'm available for the job.

Looking to the future, we can see either a dire forecast of an overexpanded, excessively expensive federal government waiting to push us into recession, even depression, at any downturn in revenues, or the possibility of a government that has been trimmed to reasonable levels with a *true surplus*, not one shaped by an accounting gimmickry.

The difference may well depend on how radically we can trim the government and cut taxes. To gauge how much waste we have described in this volume and just how much can be saved by a prudent government, please follow me as I attempt a compendium of waste, and subsequent savings.

Appendix

An Inventory of Waste: What's the Total?

No such list can be exactly accurate, but we will attempt to estimate the savings that could come from efficient government as I have already explained in this volume.

We will start with the major savings in the A-to-Z category, then move on to waste that is detailed in Part Three.

The chart will first list the category, then the estimated waste, with the difference going to the budget's bottom line.

Each figure is per annum, and well rounded out for easier digestion.

PART ONE—NEW WASHINGTON WASTE

Accounting. . . . . *10 billion*
Computers . . . . *5 billion*
Conventions . . . . *26 million*
Corporate Welfare . . . . *75 billion*
Earned Income Tax Credit . . . . *7 billion*
Federal Palaces . . . . *1 billion*

International Funds . . . . *150 million*
Junkets . . . . *1 million*
Kickbacks and Fraud. . . . . *2 billion*
Loans. . . . . *5 billion*
Mass Transit . . . . *4 billion*
Merchant Marine . . . . *300 million*
Metric System. . . . . *1 million*
National Parks . . . . *300 million*
Peanuts . . . . *1 billion*
Pork. . . . . *15 billion*
Small-Business Criminals. . . . . *50 million*
SSI. . . . . *7 billion*
Telephones . . . . *500 million*
Universal Service Fund. . . . . *100 million*
Volunteers (AmeriCorps). . . . . *500 million*
Welfare . . . . *100 billion*
Youth at Risk. . . . . *3 billion*

PART TWO—REVIEW AND DÉJÀ VU

Government Aircraft . . . . *1 billion*
Decorating. . . . . *1 billion*
Mining Law of 1872 . . . . *2 billion*
Rural Utilities Services. . . . . *1 billion*
Essential Air . . . . *100 million*
Federal Employees. . . . . *42 billion*
Overhead Reduction of
    Smaller Government . . . . *35 billion*
Congressional Retirement. . . . . *50 million*
Newsletters . . . . *45 million*
Forest Service . . . . *150 million*

PART THREE—BLUEPRINT FOR THE TWENTY-FIRST CENTURY

Cabinet Consolidation and Elimination . . . 35 billion
Appalachian Regional Commission. . . . . 1 billion
Agency for International Development . . . . . 1 billion
Export-Import Bank . . . . 1 billion
Overseas Private Investment
*   Corporation . . . . 200 million*
Small Business Administration . . . . 1 billion
Sale of Power Marketing . . . . 1 billion
New Land Moratorium. . . . . 200 million
Marketing Promotion . . . . 100 million
Demo Projects for Highways . . . . 750 million
Community Development Block Grants . . . . 4 billion
Economic Development Initiatives
*   of HUD . . . . 300 million*
Disaster Relief for Private Groups and
*   Recreation. . . . . 300 million*
Duplication and Overlap. . . . . 10 billion

GRAND TOTAL OF WASTE PER YEAR IN THE FEDERAL GOVERNMENT . . . $375 BILLION

One of the reasons government waste is so large, as are our taxes, is that the public first gains, then loses, the determination to make real change in government.

The frustration among voters leaves the playing field to politicians, who are of a different stripe than ordinary hard-working citizens. They have mastered the rhetoric, with grand promises and rationalizations, that seems to appease and/or thwart those who believe in good government.

Occasionally there appears to be a revolution, which then defuses into a skirmish, then disappears entirely.

This is not true among a minority of citizens who cannot be taken in, but their power is weakened by the majority of Americans—who either do not vote or who yield to the blandishment of Washington. Professionals in the Beltway have mastered the art of taking an excessive portion of our income, for which they promise a Nirvana that never comes. Individual effort, not government, creates the wealth that makes the nation what it is.

In the boom years of 1995–2000, the wealth was created by a computer-aided increase in labor productivity, along with corporate restructuring and a well-run Federal Reserve interest-balancing regimen.

The object lesson in this is simple: we should obey Jefferson's credo that:

A WISE AND FRUGAL GOVERNMENT WHICH SHALL RESTRAIN MEN FROM INJURING ONE ANOTHER, WHICH SHALL LEAVE THEM OTHERWISE FREE TO REGULATE THEIR OWN PURSUITS OF INDUSTRY AND IMPROVEMENT, AND SHALL NOT TAKE FROM THE MOUTH OF LABOR THE BREAD THAT IT HAS EARNED— THIS IS THE SUM OF GOOD GOVERNMENT.

Index

Acadia National Park, 126
accounting errors, 9–15, *see also* specific
    agencies; departments
Advanced Micro Devices, 43
Advanced Technology Program (ATP),
    42–44
  elimination of, 261
Advanced Weather Interactive Processing
    System (AWIPS), 33–34, 67
advertising, radio and newspaper, 160–62
AFDC. *See* Aid to Families with
    Dependent Children
Agency for International Development
    (AID), 85, 260
  failures of, 69
Agriculture, Department of (USDA), 17
  computer systems, 34
  downsizing problems in, 67
  fraud and abuse of telephone services,
    187–88
  fraud in "Risk Management" division
    of, 99
  Market Access Program (MAP), 44, 261
  pork, 142
AID. *See* Agency for International
    Development
Aid to Families with Dependent Children
    (AFDC), 197, 200
airplanes, government owned nonmilitary,
    217–19
  number of, 218
Airport Trust Fund, 230
Albert, Carl, 216

American Barrick, 224
American Enterprise Institute, 59
AmeriCorps
  elimination of, 261
  mismanagement of, 193–96
Andrews Air Force Base, golf courses, 78
Antisubsidy Act, 262
Appalachian Regional Commission, 142,
    260
Archer, Bill, 274
Association of Concerned Taxpayers, 245
AT&T, 43
ATP. *See* Advanced Technology Program
AWIPS. *See* Advanced Weather Interactive
    Processing System

Babbitt, Bruce, 224
Bakersfield Californian, 175
Balanced Budget Act of 1997, 24, 50, 177
Balkanski, Alex, 41
Bandow, Doug, 86–87
Barrons magazine, 46
Bentsen, Lloyd, 61
Berthoud, John, 190
Bielski, Mike, 220
BLM. *See* Land Management, Bureau of
Boeing, 45
Border Volunteer Corp. (BVC), 195
Breyer, Stephen, 72
bribery. *See* fraud
bridge tolls, 110
Bryan, Richard, 226
budget legislation, 22

budget surplus, fallacy of, 3–4, 19–30, 208
  legislation exposing, 28–29
  national debt figures and, 24–27
  origin of, 23–24
  stock market crash and, 21
  trust-fund monies and, 21–24, 26, 29–30
Bumpers, Dale, 225
Burke, Vee, 198
Bush, George, 29, 123, 232
BVC. *See* Border Volunteer Corp.
Byrd, Robert C., 75, 146

cabinet agencies
  independent, 260
  reorganization of, 254–60
  semiautonomous, 260
CACFP. *See* Child and Adult Care Food
  Program
Calder, Philip T., 12
Campbell Soup Co., 44
Carnival Cruise Lines, 115
Carter, Jimmy, 137
"Cash and Noncash Benefits for Persons
  with Limited Income," 198
Caterpillar, 43
CATO Institute, 42, 86–87
C-Cube Microsystems, Inc., 41
Census Bureau, 201
Chief Financial Officers Act, 12
Child and Adult Care Food Program
  (CACFP), 16–18
childhood disability
  definition of, 174
  Supplemental Security Income (SSI) and,
    172–74, 262
Chrysler Corporation, 46
CIO system, criteria for, 35–36
Citizens Against Government Waste, 27, 42,
  91, 153, 236
Citizens for a Sound Economy, 191
Clean Coal Technology, corporate welfare
  and, 47
Clinger-Cohen Act of 1996, 35, 36
Coca-Cola, 46
Cohen, William S., 32
Colgan Airways, 229
Commerce, Department of, 123
  Advanced Technology Program (ATP),
    42–44, 261
  metric system and, 121–24, 262
  National Institute of Science and
    Technology, 125
  National Weather Service, 33–34, 66–67
  reorganization of, 257
Committee on Transportation and
  Infrastructure, 50
Commodity Credit Corporation, 139

Communities Act of 1994 program, 207
Community Development Block Grants, 142
  elimination of, 261
"Computer Chaos: Billions Wasted Buying
  Federal Computer Systems" report, 32
computer systems
  mismanagement of, 31–37
  see also specific agencies; departments
con jobs. *See* fraud
concessions, national park, 126–28
Concessions Act of 1965, 127
Concord Coalition, 27–28
  New York Times ad, 29–30
Congress, reforms needed in, 264–67
Congressional Budget Office, 26
Congressional Research Service, 198
Consolidated Financial Statements of the
  United States Government, 12–13
consumer price index (CPI), 183
Contract with America Advancement Act,
  175
corporate welfare, 41–48
  Advanced Techology Program (ATP) as,
    42–44
  Antisubsidy Act and, 262
  beneficiaries of, 43, 44–45
  cash subsidies, grants, loans, and tax
    loopholes as, 46–47
  Forest Service and, 240–42
  Market Access Program (MAP) as, 44
  solutions, 47
  underwriting of business loans as,
    45–46
courthouses, federal appropriations for,
  72–73, 74–77
Cox, Wendell, 111
CPI. *See* consumer price index
credit card fraud, 93
criminals, Small Business Administration
  (SBA) loans to, 167–69
Cypress Viaduct, 158–59

day care, unwilling recipients of money for,
  16–18
DDI. *See* Direct Deposit Indicator
DEA. *See* Drug Enforcement Administration
debt securities, 22
DeConcini, Dennis, 80
decorating programs, General Services
  Administration (GSA) and, 219–21
DeFazio, Peter, 79, 80
Defense, Department of, 255
  accounting errors, 10–11
  computer systems, 31, 33, 34
  congressional junkets, 89–92
  as fraud victim, 100–1
  golf courses, 78–80, 262

personnel reductions, 232, 233
pork, 142
Defense Finance and Accounting Service
    (DFAS), 11
Delaware Water Gap National Recreation
    Area, outhouses, 135–36, 153
demonstration projects for highways, 49–56
    elimination of, 261
Department of Agriculture and Rural
    Development Appropriations Act, 226
DFAS. *See* Defense Finance and Accounting
    Service
Digital Equipment, 43
Direct Deposit Indicator (DDI), 62–63
disaster relief
    reorganization of, 262
    waste in, 155–59
DOE. *See* Energy, Department of
DOT. *See* Transportation, Department of
Drug Enforcement Administration (DEA),
    telephone services in, 188–89
DuPont, 43

Earned Income Tax Credit (EITC), 57–64,
    198
    fraud concerning, 61–63, 101
    as "free money," 57–58
    inequities of, 59–61
    solutions, 63–64
Eastman Kodak, 43
Economic Development Initiatives (EDI), 142
    elimination of, 262
EDI. *See* Economic Development Initiatives
Education, Department of
    accounting errors, 14
    computer systems, 34–35
    defaulted student loans, 68, 107
Eisenhower, Dwight D., 271
EITC. *See* Earned Income Tax Credit
employees, federal
    accounting problems involving, 14
    reductions in, 231–34
    salary and benefits of, 233
Energy, Department of (DOE), inefficiencies
    of, 66
environmental cleanup, accounting problems
    involving, 14
Environmental Protection Agency (EPA),
    failures of, 69–70
EPA. *See* Environmental Protection Agency
Essential Air program, 47, 229–31
    elimination of, 261
ethanol
    elimination of subsidies for, 261
    tax breaks for producers of, 46
Export-Import Bank, 45, 260
    losses, 107

FAA. *See* Federal Aviation Administration
Family Day Care Home program, 17
Farm Bill of 1996, 139
Farm Credit Administration, 260
farm loans, delinquent, 68
Farmers Home Administration, computer
    systems, 33
FEC. *See* Federal Elections Commission
Federal Aviation Administration (FAA)
    accounting errors, 13
    computer systems, 31, 32
    inefficiencies of, 70–71
Federal Communications Commission
    radio spectrum auctions, 237–38
    Universal Service Fund subsidies, 190–92
Federal Elections Commission (FEC), on
    federal funding for conventions, 39–40
Federal Emergency Management Agency
    (FEMA), mismanagement of funds by,
    155–59
federal government
    cost of, 2
    errors and inefficiences of, 9–15, 65–71
    see also specific agencies; departments
Federal Highway Administration, 54, 123
Federal Housing Administration (FHA),
    losses, 107
Federal Program Management, 220
Federal Railroad Administration, 260
Federal Telecommunications Service 2000
    (FTS2000), 186
Federal Transit Administration, 260
Federal Triangle Project, 73
FEMA. *See* Federal Emergency Management
    Agency
FHA. *See* Federal Housing Administration
FICA taxes
    budget surplus and, 20–30
    increases in, 3
    see also Social Security system
Fish and Wildlife Service, 68
Foley, Tom, 216, 235
food safety, inconsistency in monitoring,
    65–66
food stamps program, 198
    fraud and abuse in, 67–68, 102, 103–5
Ford Motor Company, 46
Forest Service, 68, 218
    accounting errors, 13
    corporate welfare and, 240–42
    timber road building, 47, 262
Fossil Energy Research and Development,
    corporate welfare and, 46
Foxwoods, 132
Franking Commission, 161
    guidebook, 162
franking privileges, congressional, 161, 238

fraud, 93–105
    credit card, 93
    in Department of Justice, 96–98
    Earned Income Tax Credit (EITC), 61–63,
        101
    food stamps program, 67–68, 102, 103–5
    in General Services Administration (GSA),
        94–96
    Medicaid, 102–3
    Medicare, 102–3
    outside scams, 99–105
    pork as, 142
    in "Risk Management" division of
        Department of Agriculture, 99
    Social Security, 98–99, 101–2
    Supplemental Security Income (SSI),
        171–80
    telephone services, 187–88
FTS2000. *See* Federal Telecommunications
    Service 2000

Gallo wines, 44
gambling casinos, Native Americans, 132–34
GAO. *See* General Accounting Office
gas taxes, federal, 54–55, 111
gasahol
    elimination of subsidies for, 261
    tax breaks for producers of, 46
General Accounting Office (GAO), 10–15,
    33, 43, 65, 76, 87, 117, 129, 176, 205,
    206, 277
General Agreement to Borrow, corporate
    welfare and, 47
General Motors, 43, 46
General Services Administration (GSA)
    computer systems, 31
    fraud in, 94–96
    outside scams and, 99–105
    telecommunications services and, 186
Gingrich, Newt, 216–17
Glenn, John, 251–52
Goldstrike Mine, 224
golf courses, military, 78–80
    elimination of, 262
Gore, Al, 221, 251–52
*The Government Racket: Washington Waste
    from A to Z* (Gross), 1
government reorganization
    Antisubsidy Act, 262
    cabinet agencies, 254–60
    Congress, 264–67
    duplication and overlap, 262–64
    federal programs, 261–62
    independent inspector general, 277–79
    Initiative system, 275–76
    need for, 251–54
    pork, 267–68

presidential primaries, 268–72
    Referendum, 276–77
    taxation, 272–74
government-business partnerships, 42
Grace Commission, on government
    accounting systems, 10
Grassley, Charles E., 118
Greenspan Committee, 23
Grey, Mike, 175
GSA. *See* General Services Administration

Hansen, Clifford, 83
Hastert, Dennis, 217
HCFA. *See* Health Care Financing
    Administration
Health Care Financing Administration
    (HCFA), policy deficiencies of, 65
Health and Human Services, Department of
    reorganization of, 259
    statistical services, 182
Helium Privatization Act, 222
helium production, government expenditure
    on, 221–22
The Heritage Foundation, 42, 183
Highway Trust Fund, 55
highways, demonstration projects for, 49–56
    elimination of, 261
The Hill, 91
Hobson, David, 54
Holland-American Line, 115
Hollings, Ernest F. (Fritz), 20, 30
    on budget surplus, 28–29
Holt, Tom, 17
horse adoption plan, 81–83
House Agriculture Committee, 91
House Budget Committee, 19, 165
House Committee on Government Reform
    and Oversight, 35
House Recording Studio, 164
Housing and Urban Development,
    Department of (HUD)
    accounting errors, 13
    computer systems, 34
    internal weaknesses in, 66
    Special Purpose Grants, 142
HUD. *See* Housing and Urban Development,
    Department of; Urban, Suburban, and
    Rural Affairs, Department of

IBM, 43
immigrants, Supplemental Security Income
    (SSI) and, 176–78
Immigration and Naturalization Service
    (INS), inefficiency of, 69
independent agencies, elimination of, 260
Indian Affairs, Bureau of, 129, 131
Indian Trust Funds, 129–30

Information Technology Management
　　Reform Act, 35
Initiative laws, 275–76
INS. *See* Immigration and Naturalization
　　Service
inspector general, establishing independent,
　　277–79
Intel, 43
Interior, Department of the
　　Bureau of Land Management (BLM), 68,
　　　81
　　uncoordinated and duplicated services of,
　　　68–69
Intermodal Surface Transportation Efficiency
　　Act (ISTEA), 49
Internal Revenue Service (IRS)
　　accounting errors, 9–10, 11–12
　　computer systems, 31, 32–33, 36
　　elimination of, 272–74
　　insufficient security controls, 71
International Bureau of Weights and
　　Measures, 122
International Enterprise Funds, 84–88
　　elimination of, 262
　　reasons for failure of, 87
　　solutions, 87–88
IRS. *See* Internal Revenue Service
ISTEA. *See* Intermodal Surface
　　Transportation Efficiency Act

Job Corps program, misleading claims
　　concerning, 70
Johnson, Lyndon B., 3
Jones Act of 1920, 118
junkets, congressional, 89–92
　　solutions, 92
Justice, Department of, fraud in, 96–98

Kasich, John, 50
Keating, David, 239
Kennedy, John F., 232
Kentucky Distillers Association, 44
Kerrey, Robert, 28
kickbacks. *See* fraud
Kosters, Marvin, 59

La Follette, Robert M., 271
Labor, Department of
　　misleading claims concerning Job Corps
　　　program, 70
　　reorganization of, 257
Land Management, Bureau of (BLM), 68, 81
Legislative Service Organizations (LSOs),
　　222–23
Livingston, Bob, 28
loan programs, 106–9
　　accounting errors, 14

　　solutions, 109
　　student, 68, 107
LSI Logic Corporation, 42
LSOs. *See* Legislative Service Organizations

M & M Mars, 45
McCain, John, 55, 76
Mack, Connie, 239
Madison, James, 5
MAP. *See* Market Access Program
Maritime Administration, 116, 117, 119,
　　120, 260
Maritime Security Program, 118–19
Market Access Program (MAP), 44
　　elimination of, 261
mass transit
　　elimination of subsidies for, 261
　　federal subsidies for, 110–14
Medicaid, 198
　　fraud concerning, 102–3
Medicare, fraud concerning, 102
member's representational allowance
　　(MRA), 161
Mercer/Foster Higgins survey, 202
merchant marine, 115–20
　　elimination of subsidies for, 261
　　federal subsidies for, 118–20
　　government stifling of, 115–18
　　solutions, 120
Metcalf, Jack, 79
Metric Board, U.S., 123
Metric Conversion Act, 123
metric system program, 121–24
　　elimination of, 262
military, accounting errors in, 10–11
Minge, David, 79
Mining Law of 1872, 223–25
　　elimination of cheap land patents under, 262
mohair subsidies, 226–27
Mohegan Sun, 132
Motorola, 43
Moynihan, Pat, 23, 28
MRA. *See* member's representational
　　allowance

Nader, Ralph, 42
National Aeronautics and Space
　　Administration, costs and schedules
　　problems, 70
national debt, 106
　　budget surplus and, 24–26, 208
　　explanation of, 26–27
　　government loan programs and, 106–9
　　increases in, 208–11
　　solutions for reducing, 211
National Endowment for the Humanities,
　　pork, 142

National Furniture Center, 219
National Helium Reserve, 221
National Institutes of Science and Technology, 124
National Park Service (NPS), 68
  mismanagement by, 125–28
  outhouse construction by, 135–36
national parks, mismanagement of, 125–28
National Science Foundation, pork, 142
National Semiconductor, 43
National Service Corporation, 193, 195–96
National Taxpayers Union, 109, 153, 190, 235, 239
National Weather Service
  computer systems, 33–34
  modernization failures in, 66–67
National Wool Act, 226
Native American Housing Assistance and Self-Determination Act, 130
Native Americans, 129–34
  gambling casinos, 132–34
  housing problems, 130–32
New York Times, 27
  Concord Coalition ad in, 29–30
newsletters, congressional, subsidies for, 238–40
NEXRAD (Next Generation Weather Radar), 67
NPS. *See* National Park Service
Nuclear Regulatory Commission, uncertainty and confusion in, 66
Nunn, Sam, 27

Ocean Spray, 44
Office of Former Speakers, 216–17
  elimination of, 261
Office of Management and Budget (OMB), 187
Office of Personnel Management, 233
OMB. *See* Office of Management and Budget
Omnibus Trade and Competitiveness Act of 1988, 123
O'Neill, Thomas "Tip," 216
"Operation Clean Sweep," 167
OPIC. *See* Overseas Private Investment Corporation
outhouses, 135–36, 153
"Outreach Demonstration Project" grants, 177
Overseas Private Investment Corporation (OPIC), 45, 46, 85, 260

Panetta, Leon, 251, 252
"Partnership for a New Generation of Vehicles," 46

Patent and Trademark Office (PTO), federal appropriations for, 73–74
peanuts
  elimination of quota system for, 262
  price supports for, 139–40
  quota system for raising and selling, 137–40
Pei, I. M., 72
Pena, Federico, 218
pensions, congressional, 235–36
perks, congressional, 242–48
  list of, 245–46
Peterson, Peter G., 27
Petfood Institute, 44
Pickering, Chip, 54
Pillsbury Company, 44
political conventions, elimination of, 261
pork, 141–54
  elimination of, 267–68
  examples of, 143–53
  federal programs providing, 142
  solutions, 154
  see also specific topics
poverty, eliminating, 201–3
Powell, Colin, 194
presidential conventions, federal funding for, 38–40
presidential primaries, reorganization of, 268–72
prisoners, Supplemental Security Income (SSI) and, 175–76
Progressive Policy Institute, 42
Proxmire, William, 112–13
PTO. *See* Patent and Trademark Office
Public Debt, Bureau of the, 24–26, 208

radio ads, for congressional town hall meetings, 160–62
radio spectrum auctions, 237–38
Ralston Purina, 44–45
REA. *See* Rural Electrification Administration
Reagan, Ronald, 50
recording studios, congressional, subsidized, 163–66
Referendum, 276–77
"reinventing government" plan, 252
retirement benefits, congressional, 235–36
Richardson, Margaret, 61
Roberts, Pat, 223
Rockwell, 43
Rocky Mountain National Park, 126
Rodgers, T. J., 41
Roll Call, 54
Ronald Reagan International Trade Building, federal appropriations for, 73

Roosevelt, Franklin D., 3
Rowland, John, 275
Royce, Ed, 44
Rubin, Robert E., 12
Rudman, Warren, 27
Rural Electrification Administration (REA), 227
Rural Utilities Services, 227–29
  corporate welfare and, 47
  elimination of, 261

S & L insurance bailout, 107
Safe and Drug Free Schools program, 207
Santorum, Rick, 139
Sasser, James R., 218
SBA. *See* Small Business Administration
Schatz, Tom, 27, 91, 236
Schroeder, Pat, 235
Schuster, Harvey, 86
Seattle Times, 131
Sematech, 42
Senate Committee on Governmental Operations, 251
Senate Ethics Committee, 243
Senate Recording Studio, 164
Senate S-21 bill, 28
Senate Select Committee on Intelligence, 91
Shaiko, Ronald, 244
Shays, Christopher, 79, 139, 243
Shell Petroleum, 43
Shuster, Bud, 49–50, 54
Small Business Administration (SBA), 45, 167–70
  elimination of, 260
  loans to criminals, 167–69
Smith, Linda, 243
Snyder, Tom, 252
Social Security system
  accounting errors, 14
  budget surplus and, 20–30
  fraud in, 98–99, 101–2
  tax increases, 3
Speaker of the House, former, perks, 216–17
SSI. *See* Supplemental Security Income
statistical services
  duplication and overlap in, 181–84
  major, 182
  solutions, 183–84
Stockman, Steve, 161
student loans, 68, 107
Stuyvesant High School, 37
substance abusers, Supplemental Security Income (SSI) and, 174–75
Sullivan v. Zebley, 173–74
Summers, Lawrence, 33

Supplemental Security Income (SSI), 171–80, 198
  childhood disability cases and, 172–74, 262
  ease of scamming, 171–72
  immigrants and, 176–78
  prisoners and, 175–76
  solutions, 179–80
  substance abusers and, 174–75

Taft, Robert, 271
TANF. *See* Temporary Assistance for Needy Families
Tauzin, Billy, 274
Tax Foundation, 2
Tax Freedom Day, 3
The Tax Racket (Gross), 274
taxation, 2–3
  reform proposals concerning, 272–74
Taxpayer's Liability Index (TLI), 109
Taylor, Sid, 109
TEA-21. *See* Transportation Equity Act for the Twenty-First Century
telephone companies
  long-distance costs, 191–92
  Universal Service Fund (USF) subsidies for, 190–92
telephone service, 185–89
  long-distance expenditures, 186
Temporary Assistance for Needy Families (TANF), 172, 200
terrorism, combating, waste and inefficiency in, 66
Texas Instruments, 43
TLI. *See* Taxpayer's Liability Index
Toward a Metric America program, 123
town hall meetings, radio ads for, 160–62
Toyota, 46
Transportation, Department of (DOT), 217
  pork, 142
Transportation Equity Act for the Twenty-First Century (TEA-21), 51–53, 55, 111, 112
Treasury, Department of, 208, *see also* Internal Revenue Service
Treaty of the Meter, 122
Truman, Harry S., 3, 232
TRW, 43
20/20 (television program), 220
Tyson Foods, 44

UMTA. *See* Urban Mass Transit Administration
United Airlines, 43

Universal Service Fund (USF), 190–92
    elimination of, 262
    solutions, 192
    telephone companies subsidies from,
        190–92
Urban, Suburban, and Rural Affairs,
    Department of, reorganization of,
    259–60
Urban Mass Transit Administration
    (UMTA), 112–13
USDA. *See* Agriculture, Department of
USF. *See* Universal Service Fund

Veterans Affairs, Department of, computer
    systems, 35
veterans benefits, accounting problems
    involving, 14

waste, government
    inventory of, 281–84
    overview of, 1–5
    see also specific topics
Welch's, 44

Welfare, Department of, reorganization of,
    258
welfare programs, 197–203
    costs of, 198, 199
    number of, 198–99
    reform of, 200
    solutions, 200–3
    "welfare reform," 200
Welfare Reform Act of 1996, 174, 177
Wellstone, Paul, 243
White House staff, 232
WIC (Women, Infants, and Children)
        program, fraud in, 104
Wild Free Roaming Horse and Burro Act, 81
wool subsidies, 226–27
Wright, Jim, 216

Xerox, 43

youth programs, 204–7
    cost of, 205
    number of, 205
    solutions, 207